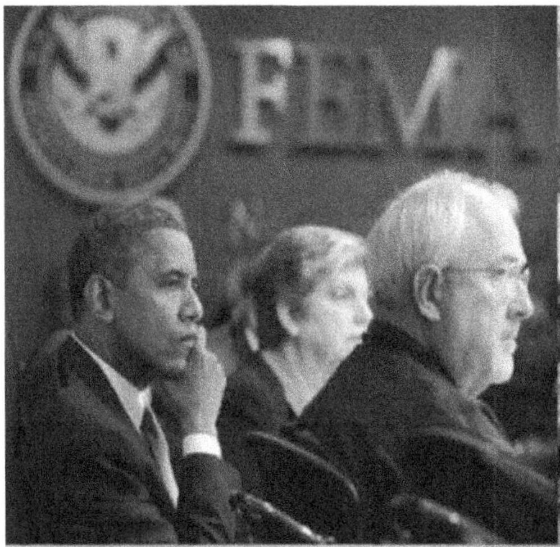

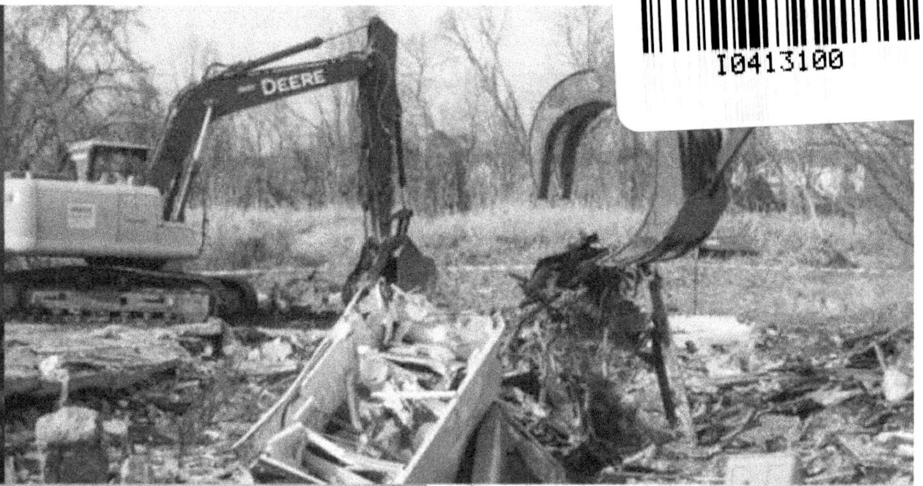

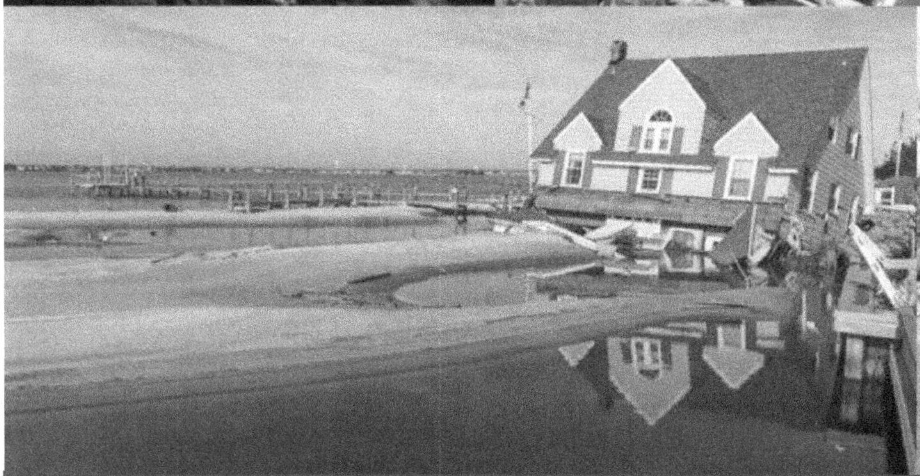

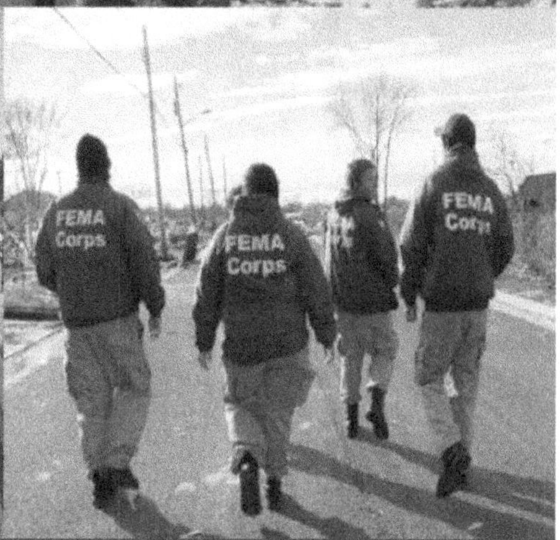

Hurricane Sandy FEMA After-Action Report

July 1, 2013

Letter from the Administrator

Team,

Over the last four years, FEMA has made continuous progress in improving our capabilities to support the Whole Community before, during, and after disasters. FEMA's performance during Sandy response and recovery operations highlighted this progress. We deployed Incident Management Assistance Team (IMAT) leaders capable of quickly identifying and solving challenges in the field. We conducted the first mass deployment of FEMA Corps, executed the inaugural activation of the Surge Capacity Force, collected and used crowd-sourced information to improve our operational efficiency, and deployed the first Innovation Team comprised of Whole Community partners. Together, these and other key accomplishments demonstrate our commitment to supporting affected communities and improving survivor outcomes.

We also recognize where work remains to further improve. We still do not go big enough, fast enough, or smart enough. Building on our experiences from Sandy, we will continue our efforts to prepare for catastrophic events and not rest on past performance. We still plan for what we are capable of doing. We still train and exercise for what we can manage. We must plan, train, and exercise even bigger to fracture the traditional mindset. We know that it is reassuring to survivors to see government representatives who are actively engaged in the area of impact. We are an organization in which every employee, full-time or temporary, has an integral role in reducing the suffering of survivors and supporting communities toward recovery.

I know that many of you have worked tirelessly over the last several months. Your efforts have made a difference and are appreciated. I spend a lot of time talking with survivors and state and local officials—they cannot say enough about the dedication and compassion of FEMA employees. Each of you has a role in this report and I am personally committed to ensuring that the opportunities to strengthen FEMA are accomplished. Now is the time to refocus on our FEMA mission and ask how—in each and everything we do—we can more efficiently and effectively meet the needs of disaster survivors.

W. Craig Fugate

FEMA Administrator

Table of Contents

Executive Summary

Introduction

Sandy, the second-largest Atlantic storm on record, affected the East Coast from Florida to Maine, as well as states as far inland as West Virginia, Ohio, and Indiana. The storm made landfall in southern New Jersey on October 29, 2012, battering the densely populated New York and New Jersey region with heavy rains, strong winds, and record storm surges. The storm's effects were extensive, leaving more than 8.5 million customers without power, causing widespread flooding throughout the region, and contributing to acute fuel shortages in parts of New York and New Jersey. The storm damaged or destroyed hundreds of thousands of homes, caused tens of billions of dollars in damages, and killed at least 162 people in the United States.

The Federal Emergency Management Agency (FEMA) coordinated a large-scale Federal response that contributed to the integrated, national effort to support affected states and communities. In the days before Sandy's landfall, FEMA worked closely with Whole Community partners— including all levels of government, private and nonprofit sectors, faith-based organizations, communities, and individuals—to prepare for the storm and anticipate survivor needs. The Agency pre-positioned commodities and assets, activated response centers, and deployed over 900 personnel ahead of Sandy's landfall. In the initial response to the storm, the Agency coordinated with its partners to provide Federal resources and to develop innovative solutions to address power restoration, transportation, fuel distribution, and housing needs. As recovery efforts began, FEMA continued to work with its partners to assist survivors and their communities. The Agency executed one of the largest deployments of personnel in its history, delivered over $1.2 billion in housing assistance to more than 174,000 survivors, and obligated over $800 million for debris removal and infrastructure restoration.

Despite these successes, the response to Sandy also revealed notable challenges in how FEMA coordinates with its Federal partners, supports state and local officials and disaster survivors, integrates with the Whole Community, and prepares and deploys its workforce. Difficulties with issuing timely mission assignments, the implementation of incident management structures, and meeting survivor needs early in the response phase are examples of challenges that emerged during Sandy. Addressing these and other issues is a near-term priority for FEMA and its partners in order to improve response and recovery operations in future disasters. Ultimately, the Sandy experience demonstrated significant progress achieved in recent years, but also confirmed that larger-scale incidents will stress the Agency's capacity for effective response and recovery.

Strengths and areas for improvement

FEMA established the Sandy Analysis Team to review all aspects of the Agency's preparations for, immediate response to, and initial recovery from the storm. The Sandy Analysis Team analyzed a wide variety of data and supporting information from FEMA and its Whole Community partners. Based on this analysis, the Sandy Analysis Team identified strengths and areas for improvement organized across four overarching themes.

Theme 1: Ensuring unity of effort across the Federal response

In response to Sandy, FEMA coordinated a large-scale mobilization of Federal teams, supplies, and other assets both before and immediately after landfall. The magnitude of the disaster revealed several strengths and areas for improvement related to integrating and coordinating Federal operations.

Strengths and Areas for Improvement

- **Strength:** The President expedited Federal disaster declarations
- **Strength:** Using an online crisis management system to coordinate Federal response operations
- **Area for Improvement:** Integrating Federal senior leader coordination and communications into response and recovery operations
- **Area for Improvement:** Coordinating Emergency Support Functions (ESFs) and Recovery Support Functions (RSFs) to support disaster response and recovery
- **Area for Improvement:** Refining the mission assignment process
- **Area for Improvement:** Implementing incident management structures
- **Area for Improvement:** Using planning and analysis to drive operational decision-making
- **Area for Improvement:** Ensuring continuous improvement of disaster doctrine, policies, and plans

Theme 2: Being Survivor-Centric

Responding to and recovering from disasters is ultimately about meeting survivors' needs. In the wake of Sandy, FEMA established a large field presence of deployed personnel who innovated to reach more survivors and improve their experiences with the Agency. While these efforts eased the recovery process for many individuals, opportunities remain to better serve survivors' needs.

Strengths and Areas for Improvement

- **Strength:** Meeting survivor needs through innovation
- **Area for Improvement:** Meeting survivors' needs during initial interactions
- **Area for Improvement:** Ensuring survivors have equal access to services
- **Area for Improvement:** Reducing the complexity of the Public Assistance program

Theme 3: Fostering unity of effort across the Whole Community

FEMA's response and recovery operations are most effective when implemented in concert with Whole Community activities. During Sandy, FEMA demonstrated progress in integrating its response and recovery efforts with the Whole Community. As the Agency prepares for the full range of potential disasters, FEMA recognizes that it must continue to improve efforts to work with community members before incidents occur and integrate Whole Community partners during incident response and recovery.

Strengths and Areas for Improvement

- **Strength:** Integrating response and recovery efforts with nongovernmental partners
- **Area for Improvement:** Coordinating among states, localities, and tribes

Theme 4: Developing an agile, professional emergency management workforce

FEMA completed one of the largest personnel deployments in its history, at a time when major efforts to transform the disaster workforce were still under way. To meet Sandy staffing needs, FEMA leveraged elements of this incomplete transformation—including new sources of personnel that were established to meet force structure requirements. The Agency also tested a new credentialing system for positions within that force structure. Given that the workforce transformation is incomplete, Sandy revealed challenges in FEMA's ability to deploy sufficient numbers of credentialed personnel for a large incident. The response also illustrated that large-scale incidents create challenges for the Agency in areas such as lodging, travel, and information technology when it is supporting a large deployed workforce. Further, large deployments create challenges for maintaining steady-state functions.

Strengths and Areas for Improvement

- **Strength:** Completing one of the largest and most diverse personnel deployments in FEMA history

- **Area for Improvement:** Ensuring a qualified disaster workforce

- **Area for Improvement:** Mobilizing the FEMA workforce for disaster response

- **Area for Improvement:** Supporting deployed personnel

- **Area for Improvement:** Ensuring continuity of operations

Next steps

While Sandy's effects were devastating, FEMA must prepare for incidents that are larger and more complex. The strengths and areas for improvement presented in this report are crucial for improving FEMA's ability to respond to and recover from future incidents. In accordance with the Agency's LL/CIP, FEMA components will be responsible for implementing, tracking, and reporting on areas for improvement. FEMA has established a Continuous Improvement Working Group (CIWG), which met for the first time in February 2013, to assign and monitor continuous improvement actions that reach beyond a single component or that have FEMA-wide implications.

In recognition of the importance of the findings in this report, FEMA has already begun to address a number of the areas for improvement. For example, FEMA has convened an Executive Steering Committee to update the mission assignment process and is adding functionality to its crisis management system to increase transparency of the status of mission assignments. The Agency also updated its *Incident Management Handbook* in January 2013 to clarify command relationships across its numerous field structures and enhance coordination with state, local, territorial, and tribal partners. Together with the ongoing focus of the CIWG, these actions demonstrate FEMA's commitment to learning lessons from response and recovery operations, developing solutions to identified issues, and following through on their implementation in the interest of better serving disaster survivors.

Introduction

On the evening of October 29, 2012, Sandy made landfall in southern New Jersey. Sandy was the second-largest Atlantic storm on record, with effects felt across 24 states. The storm battered the East Coast, particularly the densely populated New York, New Jersey, and Connecticut region, with heavy rain, strong winds, and record storm surges, and with heavy snowfall in West Virginia and the Appalachian Mountains. In Sandy's immediate aftermath, over 23,000 people sought refuge in temporary shelters, and over 8.5 million customers were left without power. The storm flooded numerous roads and tunnels and blocked transportation corridors, contributing to fuel shortages across the New York metropolitan area.

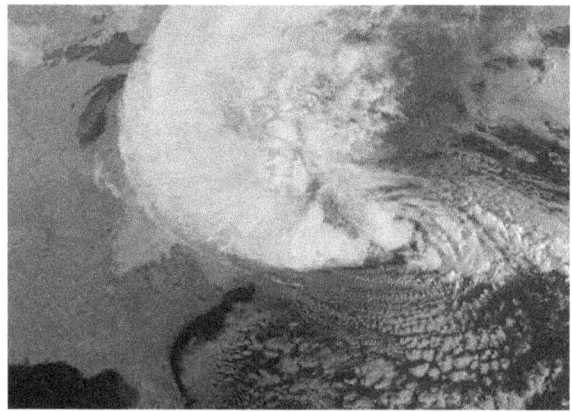

Figure 1: Sandy's impacts were felt across 24 states.

Ultimately, the storm caused tens of billions of dollars in damages, damaged or destroyed hundreds of thousands of homes, and killed at least 162 people in the United States.

The Federal Emergency Management Agency (FEMA) provided resources to support the Whole Community—including local, tribal, and state partners; nongovernmental organizations; and individual families—in its response to the storm. In the days before the storm hit, the Agency worked with threatened communities to develop incident response plans and pre-position supplies to support response efforts. Immediately after the storm, FEMA coordinated Federal resources to assist Whole Community life-saving measures and stabilization efforts. The Agency moved to meet long-term survivor needs, working with state, tribal, local, public, disability community, and private partners on housing solutions, as well as providing over $1.2 billion in aid.

Sandy response and recovery efforts demonstrated key strengths. The President expedited disaster declarations, speeding Federal response and recovery support to affected states, localities, and tribes. In addition, FEMA and its Federal partners used an online crisis management system to facilitate unity of effort across the Federal response. FEMA also identified and implemented innovative approaches and worked closely with Whole Community partners to support response and recovery operations. Finally, FEMA drew upon a variety of new programs to complete one of the Agency's largest and most diverse deployments of personnel to date.

Despite these strengths, the scale and severity of the storm created significant challenges regarding restoration of power and transportation systems, fuel availability, and housing. Through these challenges, FEMA identified opportunities to further improve how it coordinates with Federal partners, serves disaster survivors, integrates with Whole Community partners, and prepares and deploys its workforce.

In January 2013, Congress passed the Sandy Recovery Improvement Act of 2013 (part of the broader Disaster Relief Appropriations Act), which the President then signed. Legislative changes allow FEMA—and the state, local, and tribal governments it supports—greater flexibility in administering assistance programs, improving the Nation's ability to efficiently respond to and recover from disasters.

While the effects of Sandy were devastating, FEMA recognizes that it must plan and prepare for even more severe events. FEMA is committed to continuous improvement and ensuring that future response and recovery operations incorporate the lessons learned and best practices identified during Sandy.

> **Sandy Recovery Improvement Act**
>
> On January 29, 2013, President Obama signed into law the Sandy Recovery Improvement Act of 2013 (P.L. 113-2) (SRIA). The law authorizes several significant changes to the way FEMA may deliver disaster assistance under a variety of programs. These programs include Public Assistance, Permanent Work procedures, debris removal, Hazard Mitigation, dispute resolution, Federal Assistance to Individuals and Households, adds additional reviews for certain types of projects, and amends the Stafford Act to provide for an option for the Chief Executive of a federally recognized Indian tribe to make a direct request to the President for a major disaster or emergency declaration. FEMA is currently working to implement the changes authorized by SRIA.

This report was written following response and initial recovery efforts to Hurricane Sandy. Any recommendations or findings that result from other interagency Sandy-related efforts will continue to be reviewed.

Scope of the report

At the direction of FEMA Administrator Craig Fugate, the Agency established the Sandy Analysis Team to review all aspects of the Agency's preparations for, immediate response to, and initial recovery from the storm. This report contains the findings of that review. While FEMA coordinates disaster response and recovery efforts across the Federal Government and works closely with non-Federal Whole Community partners, this report focuses on identified strengths and areas for improvement within FEMA. The analyses detailed in the report concentrate on FEMA activities in New York and New Jersey, where the scale and severity of Sandy's impacts most stressed the Agency's capabilities. By examining the events in these states, the Agency can identify where and how it must improve.

Report methodology

The Sandy Analysis Team, as the coordinator of the Sandy after-action review, examined a wide variety of input from FEMA and its Whole Community partners. The team's approach included:

- Developing an event chronology that catalogs over 1,500 specific decisions, actions, and events related to the response to- and initial recovery from the storm;

- Developing and analyzing 44 quantitative datasets that indicate how the storm's impact, as well as the Nation's response and recovery, evolved over time;

- Analyzing 43 FEMA component submissions on lessons learned from Sandy, and supporting efforts to develop component-specific after-action reports and corrective action plans;

- Interviewing 215 personnel, including FEMA headquarters officials, field and regional personnel, representatives of other Federal departments and agencies, and state and local officials;

- Issuing a survey to over 8,600 FEMA and U.S. Department of Homeland Security (DHS) Surge Capacity Force (SCF) personnel who deployed to support the Sandy response and recovery, and analyzing the 2,641 responses received;

- Coordinating 11 working groups with 121 representatives from across FEMA components that reviewed preliminary findings; and

- Inviting Whole Community partners to share their experiences and lessons learned through FEMA's *Lessons Learned Information Sharing (LLIS.gov)* system.

The Sandy Analysis Team reviewed and analyzed all of these sources to identify strengths and areas for improvement.

Organization of the report

This report begins with an overview of the storm and the response and recovery efforts. The report is then organized according to the following four themes:

- Ensuring unity of effort across the Federal response;

- Being survivor-centric;

- Fostering unity of effort across the Whole Community; and

- Developing an agile, professional emergency management workforce.

For each of these themes, this report

Core capabilities

The 2011 *National Preparedness Goal* establishes 31 core capabilities that are most essential to the Whole Community in order to prevent, protect against, mitigate the effects of, respond to, and recover from the types of incidents that pose the greatest risk to the Nation.

Because integrating and coordinating the Whole Community is such an important part of FEMA's role in disaster response and recovery efforts, many of the report's identified strengths and areas for improvement pertain to the Operational Coordination core capability. Other relevant core capabilities referenced include: Planning; Public Information and Warning; Infrastructure Systems; Economic Recovery; and Housing.

---

identifies strengths and areas for improvement. Throughout the report, call-out boxes highlight Whole Community innovations that emerged during Sandy.[1] These innovations demonstrate how FEMA response and recovery operations work in concert with the activities of the Whole Community.

---

[1] References to specific Whole Community partners do not constitute endorsements of the organization or its services.

Overview of the Storm, its Impacts, and the Response

Sandy's path

Sandy was the 18th named storm of the 2012 Hurricane Season and the 10th hurricane. The storm formed in the southwestern Caribbean Sea on October 22 and became a hurricane two days later. After passing through Cuba as a Category 2 hurricane on October 25, Sandy weakened to a Category 1 hurricane and moved north over the Atlantic Ocean, parallel to the southeastern United States. As the storm moved north, it merged with an arctic cold front. This steered it to the northwest and gave Sandy its extremely broad wind field. The storm produced severe flooding along the Atlantic Coast, blizzard-like conditions in the Appalachian Mountains (with more than two feet of snow in areas of West Virginia, Virginia, Maryland, and North Carolina), and extreme winds and localized flooding in the coastal areas of the Great Lakes.

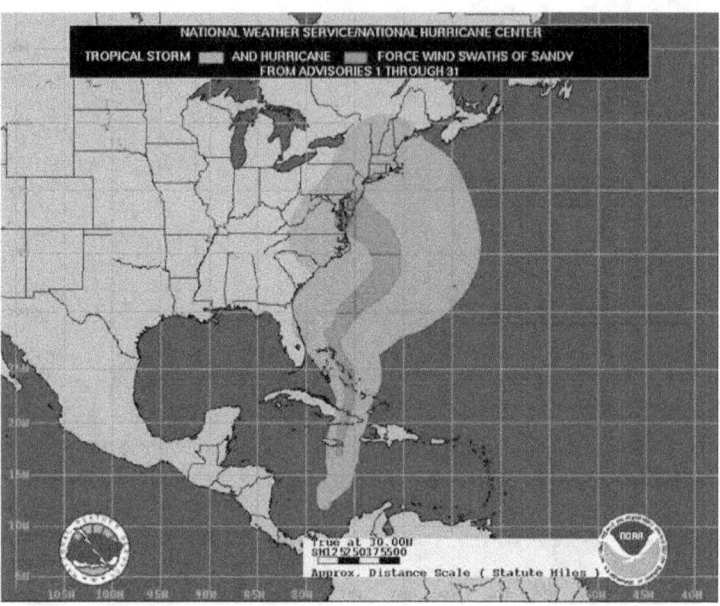

Figure 2: Sandy made landfall near Atlantic City, NJ on October 29, 2012 as a post-tropical cyclone after traveling up the southeastern U.S. coast as a Category 1 hurricane.

On the morning of October 29, the combination of a high-pressure pattern over New England and a mid-level trough moving east from the Midwest redirected the storm's trajectory toward southern New Jersey. Sandy made landfall later that evening near Atlantic City, New Jersey, as a post-tropical cyclone with hurricane-force winds of up to 80 miles per hour. The storm weakened as it moved west across southern Pennsylvania on October 30. By November 1, most of the wind and rains from the storm's remnants had diminished across the affected states. Figure 2 shows the storm's path from formation to landfall.

With tropical storm–force winds extending 580 miles from the center, Sandy was the second-largest Atlantic storm on record. The storm affected the East Coast from Florida to Maine, as well as states as far inland as West Virginia, Ohio, and Indiana. Sandy particularly lashed the New York and New Jersey coasts with heavy rain, winds, and a record storm tide that approached 14 feet in some areas. The storm's impact was intensified because it made landfall in the most populated region of the country—a region that includes critical infrastructure vital to the Nation's economy.

Preparations for Sandy

In the days leading up to Sandy's landfall, FEMA and the Whole Community made extensive preparations for the storm. FEMA based pre-landfall decisions both on the predictions of the storm's track and intensity, as well as on requests from states expecting to be impacted. Prior regional catastrophic planning coordination between FEMA and the impacted states facilitated these decisions. Ultimately, over 900 FEMA personnel pre-deployed and were on the ground when Sandy made landfall. Key pre-landfall actions included:

- Establishing Incident Support Bases in Massachusetts and New Jersey, as well as five Federal Staging Areas in New York, to pre-position commodities, generators, and communications vehicles (pre-staged commodities included 892,000 liters of water, 561,000 meals, 11,900 blankets and cots, 183 generators, 30 infant and toddler kits, 2 Durable Medical Equipment [DME] kits, and 2 Consumable Medical Supplies [CMS] kits);

- Deploying liaison officers (LNOs) and 13 Incident Management Assistance Teams (IMATs) to emergency operations centers in Connecticut, Delaware, the District of Columbia, Maine, Maryland, Massachusetts, New Jersey, New York, Pennsylvania, Rhode Island, Virginia, and Vermont;

- Activating the National Response Coordination Center (NRCC)—the multi-agency coordination center that coordinates overall Federal support for major disasters and emergencies—to a Level 1, its highest level, as well as activating all Emergency Support Functions (ESFs) and the Regional Response Coordination Centers (RRCCs) for FEMA Regions I, II, III, and IV;

> **Emergency and major disaster declarations**
>
> The Robert T. Stafford Disaster Relief and Emergency Assistance Act authorizes the President—acting through FEMA—to issue *emergency* or *major disaster* declarations. Emergency declarations allow FEMA to provide Federal assistance for emergency measures that protect property, public health, and safety. Major disaster declarations make available additional recovery assistance that Federal agencies provide to state, local, and tribal governments, survivors, and certain nonprofit organizations.

- Deploying nine National Urban Search and Rescue Task Forces, including eight with waterborne rescue capabilities;

- Deploying all six Mobile Emergency Response System (MERS) detachments—which provide deployable, command, control, and incident communications capabilities—to 11 states across the East Coast;

- Pre-staging 165 ground ambulances and associated medical teams; and

- Deploying three Regional Disability Integration Specialists (RDISs) to coordinate with state and local partners and the disability community.

Coordinated response operations

Before the storm made landfall, the President authorized emergency declarations for Connecticut, the District of Columbia, Maryland, Massachusetts, New Jersey, and New York. On the day of Sandy's landfall, the President authorized additional emergency declarations for Delaware, Pennsylvania, Rhode Island, Virginia, and West Virginia; and for New Hampshire the next day. The President authorized major disaster declarations shortly after midnight on October 30 for New York and New Jersey, and the following afternoon for Connecticut. The President subsequently authorized major disaster declarations for nine other states and the District of Columbia. These declarations made Federal assistance available to communities and survivors in the impacted regions.

Figure 3: The Army National Guard prepares to provide supplies to survivors in Far Rockaway, NY.

While FEMA coordinates Federal response and recovery activities, the Federal Government is only part of the broader efforts of the Whole Community—including all levels of government, private and nonprofit sectors, faith-based organizations, communities, and individuals. FEMA deployed significant numbers of personnel, both before and after the storm made landfall, to support response and recovery efforts. At the peak of response and initial recovery efforts, more than 17,000 Federal personnel—including more than 7,500 FEMA staff—were deployed. In addition, states deployed over 11,000 National Guard personnel in the impacted areas.

In the first 72 hours of response operations, FEMA focused efforts on supporting first responders to save lives, maintain safety, restore power, and stabilize communities with the FEMA Administrator emphasizing response priorities as: people, power restoration, points of distribution for commodities, and pumping flooded tunnels. On October 29, the day Sandy made landfall, FEMA issued over $6.3 million in mission assignments to Federal partners, directing them to provide assets and services to support state, local, and tribal efforts. Federal assets and services included communications system restoration, debris removal, aerial imaging and surveillance, and health and medical care.

As the response unfolded, FEMA continued to provide needed commodities to the affected areas. By November 11, FEMA had shipped 20 million liters of water, 16 million meals, 1.7 million blankets, 79,000 cots, 138,000 tarps, 568 generators, 105 infant and toddler kits (capable of serving a total of 1,050 for one week), 5 DME kits (capable of serving a total of 1,250 survivors), and 4 CMS kits (capable of serving a total of 1,000 survivors for one week).

Infrastructure restoration

Sandy disrupted the energy and transportation infrastructure throughout the mid-Atlantic region. The storm left 8.5 million customers without power, severely damaged public transportation systems, and contributed to a significant fuel shortage along the East Coast. In support of an aggressive power-restoration effort, the President approved a 100 percent cost share, from October 31 to November 14, for emergency power restoration work performed by state, local, and tribal governments. FEMA coordinated Federal resources to assist state, local, and tribal authorities, including the following examples:

- **Energy**: At the President's direction, FEMA established the Energy Restoration Task Force on October 31 to better coordinate Federal, state, tribal, local, and private sector efforts to restore power as quickly as possible. Working through the Task Force, the U.S. Department of Defense (DOD) U.S. Transportation Command airlifted 229 power-restoration vehicles and 487 personnel to help New York and New Jersey restore power. These resources supplemented a massive private power restoration effort. Electric utilities executed mutual aid agreements to deploy over 70,000 workers to the affected areas—the largest ever dispatch of utilities workers. As fuel supplies and distribution became increasingly linked with access to power, the Task Force broadened its focus to address energy issues writ large.

- **Transportation**: The U.S. Army Corps of Engineers (USACE) assisted with pumping water out of flooded critical public transit assets in the greater New York City metropolitan area. By November 5, pumping and power-restoration efforts in tunnels and subways helped restore 80 percent of New York Metropolitan Transit Authority service, which had no service below 34th Street on November 1. Additionally, the President authorized a temporary 100 percent Federal cost share for emergency public transportation assistance, including emergency protective measures to secure public transportation infrastructure. This assistance funded bus service to temporarily replace the capacity provided by storm-damaged PATH train lines serving New York and New Jersey.

- **Fuel Distribution**: The Energy Restoration Task Force coordinated fuel distribution points for first responders across New York and New Jersey, and DOD provided 9.3 million gallons of fuel at the request of both states.

While FEMA's efforts helped alleviate the effects of the storm for many survivors, disruptions to the region's infrastructure systems persisted for several weeks after Sandy's landfall.

Housing

Sandy caused nearly $50 billion in property damage. FEMA employed a variety of programs and policies to support survivors who had lost power or were unable to live in their homes:

- At the request of state and local officials, FEMA developed the Sheltering and Temporary Essential Power (STEP) program, which funded emergency residential essential and necessary repairs to help survivors in New Jersey, New York, and Connecticut return to their homes quickly and safely. These repairs included repairing any disability-related home modifications (e.g., wheelchair ramps) that were damaged due to the storm. The STEP program completed more than 18,700 repairs in New York as of February 19, 2013.

- At the request of New York and New Jersey, FEMA activated the Transitional Sheltering Assistance (TSA) program to allow survivors in shelters to stay in participating hotels or motels until more suitable housing accommodations became available. More than 11,400 survivors in New Jersey and New York participated in the TSA program as of February 21, 2013.

- To address the high cost of living in the region, FEMA increased the amount of rental assistance available to survivors in New York and New Jersey to 125 percent of the published rate. The increase made an additional 3,000 rental resources available to survivors across New York and New Jersey.

- Due to the high cost of available rental resources, the length of lease agreements required in many New York counties, and other factors, FEMA and the U.S. Department of Housing and Urban Development (HUD) entered into a Sandy-specific interagency agreement to deliver the unique Disaster Housing Assistance Program (DHAP). Designed based on lessons learned from Hurricanes Katrina, Ike, and Gustav, DHAP-Sandy aimed to assist survivors find intermediate housing as they rebuilt their lives.

- FEMA used aerial damage assessments to determine which areas were inaccessible, and expedited short-term rental assistance to residents of those areas.[2]

- On November 6, FEMA convened a Hurricane Sandy Catastrophic Disaster Housing Task Force to support state-led task forces planning for survivors' temporary and long-term housing needs.

- FEMA issued a series of waivers for National Flood Insurance Program requirements to advance flood insurance payments to eligible property owners.

Federal assistance to survivors and communities

The President authorized major disaster declarations for 12 states and the District of Columbia, providing affected counties with assistance for emergency work and debris removal, as well as access to three programs that continue to help survivors and communities recover from Sandy:

- **Individuals and Households Program (IHP):** The IHP provides financial assistance and direct services to survivors to address their critical needs. It includes housing assistance and grants to cover specified expenses, such as housing repairs, temporary housing, and medical expenditures. As of February 20, 2013, FEMA has approved more than $1.2 billion in IHP assistance.

- **Public Assistance (PA):** The PA program awards grants to assist state, local, and tribal governments, as well as certain private nonprofits, with response and recovery efforts. Specifically, the PA program provides assistance for debris removal, emergency protective measures, and permanent restoration of infrastructure. As of February 20, 2013, FEMA has obligated more than $800 million in PA grants.

- **Hazard Mitigation Grant Program (HMGP):** The HMGP assists state, local, and tribal governments with implementing long-term hazard mitigation measures. These measures may include projects to reduce or eliminate losses from future disasters.

FEMA and its Federal partners also established a presence in affected communities to support survivors and help them register for Federal assistance. FEMA deployed over 1,700 personnel to explain available programs and assist survivors registering for Federal aid. The Agency also established a large presence of Disaster Recovery Centers (DRCs) to meet survivor needs, including 37 centers in New York and 35 in New Jersey. FEMA call centers supported these field elements and registered more than half of a million survivors for Federal assistance. In addition, as of February 21, 2013, FEMA had referred over 238,000 New York and New Jersey applicants to the Small Business Administration, which had granted over $5 billion in loans to disaster survivors.

---

[2] FEMA conducts Preliminary Damage Assessments with state and local officials to identify the impact, type, and extent of disaster damages and the resources needed for the affected community to recover.

FEMA and its Federal partners also quickly initiated their responsibilities under the *National Disaster Recovery Framework* (NDRF). FEMA appointed Federal Disaster Recovery Coordinators (FDRCs) and activated each of the NDRF Recovery Support Functions (RSFs) in New York and New Jersey approximately one week after landfall. These recovery coordinators are supporting state, local, and tribal partners as they identify and plan for the recovery needs of the affected areas.

In January 2013, Congress passed the Sandy Recovery Improvement Act of 2013 (P.L. 113-2), which the President then signed. Marking the most significant amendments to the Stafford Act in decades, this legislation amends several of FEMA's existing authorities relating to the PA program, assistance to individuals and households, hazard mitigation, and environmental and historic preservation reviews. The Act also allows federally recognized tribes to directly request emergency and major disaster declarations from the President, rather than submit declaration requests through states. These changes provide FEMA—and the state, local, and tribal governments that it supports—with greater flexibility in administering assistance programs. FEMA is currently working to implement the changes outlined in the Act.

The storm and FEMA's response in context

Sandy's effect was devastating—millions lost electricity, tens of thousands were displaced, and at least 162 people lost their lives in the United States. However, history demonstrates that the Nation will experience and must plan for storms of even greater magnitude than Sandy.

FEMA's goals include providing congregate shelter for 1.75 million people; providing additional mass care services (such as feeding and hydration) for another 1.75 million; and treating, stabilizing, and caring for 265,000 medical casualties. Sandy did not require a response of that magnitude. Nevertheless, the strengths and areas for improvement identified during Sandy are crucial to improve FEMA's ability to respond to and recover from future incidents, including Level 1 incidents (see below).

FEMA's definition of a Level 1 incident[3]

- An incident of such magnitude that the available assets that were designed and put in place for the response are completely overwhelmed or broken at the local, regional, or national level.

- Due to its severity, size, location, actual or potential impact on public health, welfare, and infrastructure incident requires an extreme amount of Federal assistance for response and recovery efforts for which the capabilities do not exist at any level of government.

- Incident requires extraordinary coordination among Federal, state, tribal and local entities due to massive levels and breadth of damage, severe impact or multi-state scope.

- Incident requires major involvement of FEMA, other Federal agencies (all primary ESF agencies activated), and deployment of initial response resources to support requirements of the affected state.

---

[3] *FEMA Incident Management and Support Keystone*, Page 27.

Ensuring Unity of Effort across the Federal Response

In response to Sandy, FEMA coordinated a large-scale mobilization of Federal teams, supplies, and other assets, both before and immediately after the storm's landfall. The President emphasized that the full resources of the Federal Government were available to support response and recovery operations and directed Federal departments/agencies to lean forward and cut red tape to speed assistance to survivors. FEMA coordinated

Figure 4: President Obama meets with his Cabinet at the NRCC to discuss response to Hurricane Sandy.

expedited disaster declarations for the affected states, helped to establish a task force to restore power and fuel, and accelerated rental assistance for eligible survivors. However, the magnitude of the disaster revealed several areas for improvement related to integrating and coordinating Federal operations—such as better coordinating emergency support functions and refining the mission assignment process. Addressing these areas for improvement will ensure that FEMA and its Federal partners efficiently deliver Federal support.

Strength: The President expedited Federal disaster declarations

The President issued emergency declarations for 11 states before Sandy made landfall on the evening of October 29. The President quickly issued major disaster declarations for New York, New Jersey, and Connecticut the day after the storm's landfall. Due to the magnitude of the storm, the Governors of these three states made their major disaster declaration requests verbally to the President. While such verbal requests are rare, waiving the written request requirement demonstrated the President's commitment to ensuring that the Federal Government supported response and recovery operations quickly and cut through red tape.

Strength: Using an online crisis management system to coordinate Federal response operations

During Sandy, FEMA employed WebEOC, an online crisis management system, to coordinate and support response operations at the NRCC. FEMA and its Federal partners used the system for multiple activities, including supporting resource requests from the field, coordinating Energy Restoration Task Force activities, maintaining situational awareness, monitoring and tracking national hurricane plan tasks, and tracking assistance delivered to survivors. Using a single online platform facilitated information sharing and ensured that each section of the NRCC and ESFs shared a common operating picture, contributing to a unified Federal response. In addition, WebEOC facilitated a common operating picture on the status of all orders through a live resource tracking board which consolidated information on all resources shipped to support Hurricane Sandy. Despite Sandy being one of the first implementations of the WebEOC system, more than 60 percent of NRCC personnel rated the system as "effective" or "very effective."

Sandy also showed areas where the platform can expand to provide a clearer Federal Common Operating Picture, including enhancements of real-time feeds, integration with other Situational Awareness products, and linking to the information of other Whole Community partners. FEMA plans to expand the scope of activities and processes conducted through the crisis management system and continue expanding its use in RRCCs and field locations. Additionally, FEMA is exploring ways to broaden the use of the system across the Federal Government.

Area for Improvement: Integrating Federal senior leader coordination and communications into response and recovery operations

As is typical for large-scale disasters, elected and appointed Federal senior leaders were deeply involved in coordinating Sandy response and recovery efforts. The President contacted state and local leaders before the storm's landfall and emphasized the Federal Government's commitment to supporting response and recovery efforts. The President also met with his Cabinet at the NRCC and emphasized to senior leaders the importance of coordinating Federal response activities through the NRCC.

This high volume of senior-level engagement presented occasional challenges during response and recovery operations. For example, while the *National Response Framework* (NRF) and the NDRF describe the important role of senior leaders, these frameworks do not provide guidance on establishing formal mechanisms for senior leader communications or coordination with operations centers. As Federal senior leaders worked aggressively to anticipate and address the needs of state, local, and tribal partners, these Federal partners did not always inform the NRCC of independent actions taken to support response and recovery efforts.

FEMA and its Federal partners also experienced challenges with accurately, clearly, and quickly communicating senior leaders' decisions to those responsible for implementing them and to those affected by them. For example, even though the President authorized a temporary 100 percent Federal cost share for power restoration and emergency public transportation assistance to speed the delivery of Federal resources, state and local governments did not understand the implementation of this policy. Some jurisdictions remained concerned about precisely which expenses would fall under the 100 percent Federal cost share, and therefore, hesitated to request some types of Federal assistance. For example, New Jersey received inconsistent messages on whether decontamination work at the Newark Waste Treatment Plant would be eligible for the 100 percent Federal cost share. Moreover, some local jurisdictions were not aware of the cost share adjustment in part because of inconsistent communications from state and Federal Government partners. Other jurisdictions did not understand the process for managing unfinished mission assignments when the 100 percent Federal cost share ended.

Area for Improvement: Coordinating Emergency Support Functions and Recovery Support Functions to support disaster response and recovery

The NRF describes the ESFs as "providing the greatest possible access to Federal department and agency resources regardless of which organization has those resources." The NDRF describes the purpose of RSFs as "support[ing] local governments by facilitating problem solving, improving access to resources and by fostering coordination among state and Federal agencies, nongovernmental partners, and stakeholders." ESFs and RSFs have a lead or coordinating agency but are supported by capabilities of multiple departments and agencies. The functions for which ESFs and RSFs are responsible require extensive Federal Government cooperation.

Sandy response efforts revealed that several ESF coordinating agencies have adopted a more department-centric approach to response operations, rather than the integrated functional approach prescribed by the NRF. In these instances, ESF coordinating agencies did not fully draw upon the capabilities of supporting departments and agencies.

For example, Sandy left 8.5 million customers without power and contributed to significant fuel shortages in parts of New York and New Jersey. FEMA senior leaders looked to ESF #12 (Energy)—coordinated by the U.S. Department of Energy (DOE)—to coordinate Federal efforts related to energy restoration. DOE struggled to meet this requirement and lacked the operational capability to fully engage supporting Federal departments and energy-sector partners in addressing energy-restoration challenges. To focus additional attention on these needs, the President directed DOE and FEMA to establish an Energy Restoration Task Force to increase Federal, state, local, and private sector coordination on power and fuel restoration. The Task Force achieved its objectives. However, Federal partners acknowledge that ESF #12 should have inherent capacity to coordinate across the full spectrum of relevant public- and private sector partners.

Similar challenges emerged with the newer RSFs. Nearly all RSF field coordinators were untrained in NDRF concepts prior to Sandy, and many initial reports and discussions from field coordinators focused solely on the authorities and activities of the lead/coordinating agency. Though most RSFs included actively engaged national working groups, a few struggled to convene national RSF primary/support agency meetings, and all RSFs experienced challenges convening field-based meetings with relevant recovery partners. Additionally, the RSFs struggled to involve partners who were not working within the Joint Field Office (JFO) but were expected to provide virtual support to the operation, per the draft *Recovery Federal Interagency Operational Plan*. The department-centric approach to recovery and the gaps in recovery experience affected the ability of some RSFs to provide coordinated assistance to state and local communities.

Area for Improvement: Refining the mission assignment process

FEMA uses mission assignments to direct Federal partners to conduct specific disaster response and recovery activities (Sections 402 and 502(a) of the Stafford Act are the basis for FEMA's mission assignment authority). Mission assignments—which include details on funding, managerial controls, and guidance—are work orders that FEMA issues to another Federal department or agency, directing completion of a specified task by that agency. Written mission assignments must be in place in order for FEMA to reimburse Federal departments and agencies for performing disaster-related activities. Mission assignments to FEMA's Federal partners—such as DOD, the U.S. Coast Guard (USCG), and the U.S. Department of Transportation—were vital to the Sandy response and recovery efforts.

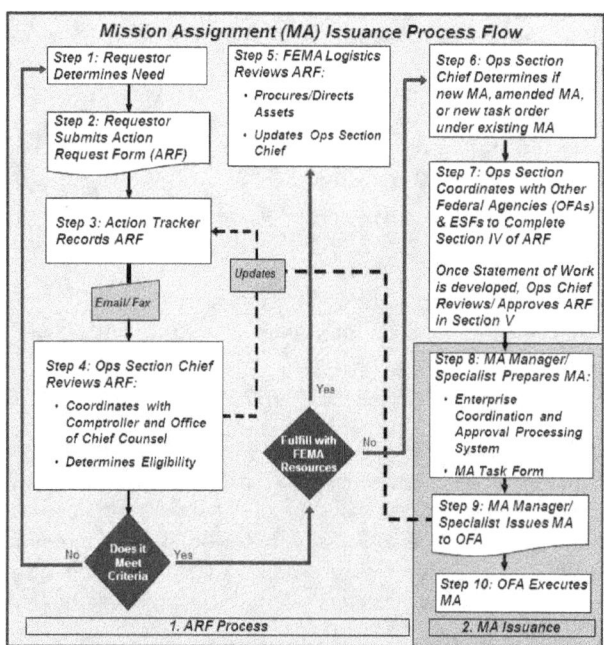

Figure 5: The mission assignment process is not optimally set up to quickly surge resources to the field in a large-scale incident.

However, the mission assignment process, outlined in Figure 5, remains complex and can be time-consuming. Approximately 40 percent of mission assignments from October 26, to November 20, took longer than one day to process. As an example, FEMA had to revise a mission assignment to the U.S. Department of Justice's Bureau of Alcohol, Tobacco, Firearms and Explosives four times to correct errors. Similarly, the U.S. Forest Service observed that some written mission assignments to ESF #4 (Firefighting) partners outlined unclear requirements while others conflicted with state requests for assistance. The willingness of several departments and agencies to act on verbal mission assignments and deploy resources before receiving a written mission assignment lessened the effect of these delays. In addition, FEMA worked with several Federal partners ahead of Sandy to develop pre-scripted mission assignments (PSMAs). These PSMAs enabled FEMA to issue clear written mission assignments to certain departments and agencies throughout the response, mitigating some of the written process delays.

Moreover, multiple response stakeholders—including states and Federal departments and agencies—can request a mission assignment. However, these response partners do not have visibility into what mission assignments other partners are requesting. Field personnel reported that this lack of transparency sometimes resulted in uncoordinated mission assignments over the course of the Sandy response.

To address these challenges, FEMA has convened an Executive Steering Committee to update the mission assignment process. In addition, FEMA's Response Directorate is adding

Figure 6: USACE employees survey the damage in Sea Bright, New Jersey.

functionality in its crisis management system to increase transparency of the status of mission assignments. Additionally, the Disaster Relief Appropriations Act now requires FEMA to post all mission assignments in excess of $1 million on the Agency's website within 24 hours of issuance.

Area for Improvement: Implementing incident management structures

Sandy response operations in New York and New Jersey revealed inconsistencies in the way FEMA establishes incident management structures for large-scale incidents. Agency doctrine gives FEMA choices of different organizational structures to meet the needs of an incident. During response efforts to Sandy, FEMA used an organizational structure that included geographical branches and divisions and an Area Coordination Group responsible for the two hardest-hit states. FEMA experienced challenges implementing these structures, which are designed for larger incidents.

Field structure for large-area incidents

FEMA's *Incident Management Handbook* provides guidance for three potential organizational constructs for disaster operations. FEMA most commonly uses a functional structure, organizing itself around the programs that it delivers. The second approach—a geographic structure—allows FEMA to organize by dividing its staff into divisions based on the geography of the affected area. The third approach—a combined organization structure—combines functional and geographic approaches. For Sandy, FEMA chose this combined organization construct for response and initial recovery activities in New York and New Jersey. This approach was designed to facilitate centralized program decision-making, while ensuring appropriate geographic coverage.

FEMA's combined organization structure helped to link the Agency's programs with local response efforts. For example, the New York and New Jersey JFOs devolved certain programs to Geographic Branch Directors and Division Supervisors who had in-depth understanding of local needs (see Figure 7 and Figure 7). FEMA's Federal Coordinating Officer (FCO) for New York cited Division Supervisors as a strength, noting that these personnel were empowered to work with local authorities to identify and meet urgent requirements. The Staten Island Borough President lauded their assigned Division Supervisor as a key source of information during response activities and critical to the establishment of a DRC on the island. FEMA's incident management structure also included efforts to deploy FEMA headquarters personnel to serve as LNOs to senior local officials. These LNOs were embedded with the leadership in selected jurisdictions and helped achieve key outcomes during response activities. For example, the Mayor of Jersey City, New Jersey, reported that their assigned LNO played a key role in the city receiving Federal resources to address survivor needs. While a number of individual LNOs were effective, LNOs as a whole were not optimally integrated into JFO operations.

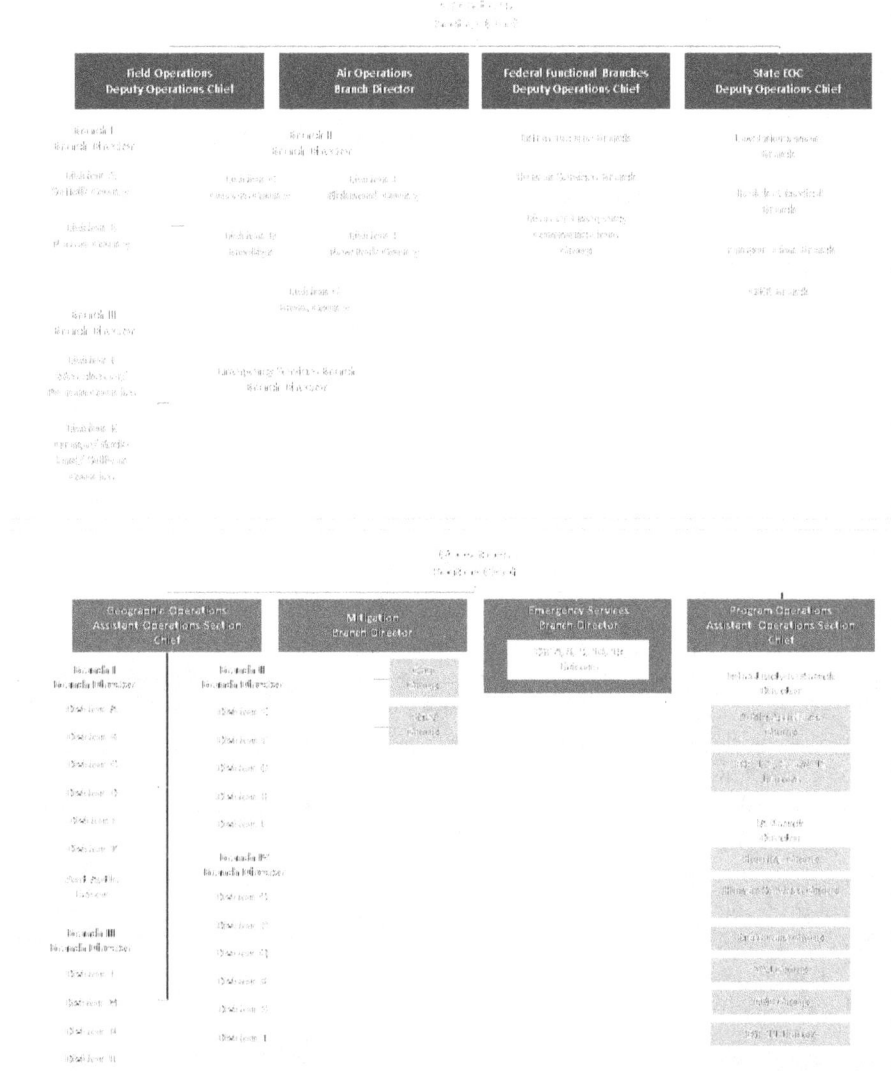

***Figure 7 and Figure 8: During Sandy, the Operations Sections at the New York and New Jersey
JFOs devolved certain programs to Geographic Branch Directors and Division Supervisors,
while centrally managing other programs.***

Despite these key successes, FEMA's implementation of the combined organization structure presented challenges in New York and New Jersey. For example, the combined organization structure created tension between program staff at the JFO (who were reluctant to decentralize their authority) and Division Supervisors and Branch Chiefs (who wanted to manage programs at the local level). Moreover, the roles and responsibilities of LNOs were unclear in relation to Division Supervisors, who had responsibility for multiple jurisdictions. Local officials reported confusion regarding who within FEMA had the authority to approve resource requests, demonstrating the need to clarify the titles, roles, responsibilities, and command relationships among Division Supervisors and LNOs.

Moreover, FEMA experienced personnel misalignments when staffing the leadership roles called for in the combined organization structure. When Sandy operations began, FEMA had 70 people whose primary position—per the FEMA Qualification System (FQS)—is to serve as Division Supervisors in the combined organization structure. Of these, 39 are fully qualified staff and 31 are trainee staff. Yet, only 10 of these FQS-qualified and FQS-trainee staff were among the 33 Division Supervisors serving in New York and New Jersey on November 8, 2012. In addition, as shown in Figure 9, the New York JFO experienced initial vacancies and high turnover while implementing the combined organization structure during the initial response. Field leadership noted that turnover in the Division Supervisor position resulted from the need to ensure that the right people were matched to the right jobs and to address misalignments quickly.

As a first step in addressing these challenges, FEMA updated its *Incident Management Handbook* in January 2013 to clarify command relationships across its numerous field structures.

Regional Response Coordination Centers

FEMA's *Incident Management and Support Keystone* states "Control of FEMA incident management and support efforts is delegated to the lowest level of execution...Delegating control in this way emphasizes a bottom-up approach to the chain of command, from the incident through the Region to FEMA Headquarters." Accordingly, the 10 FEMA Regions each have an RRCC, a standing multiagency

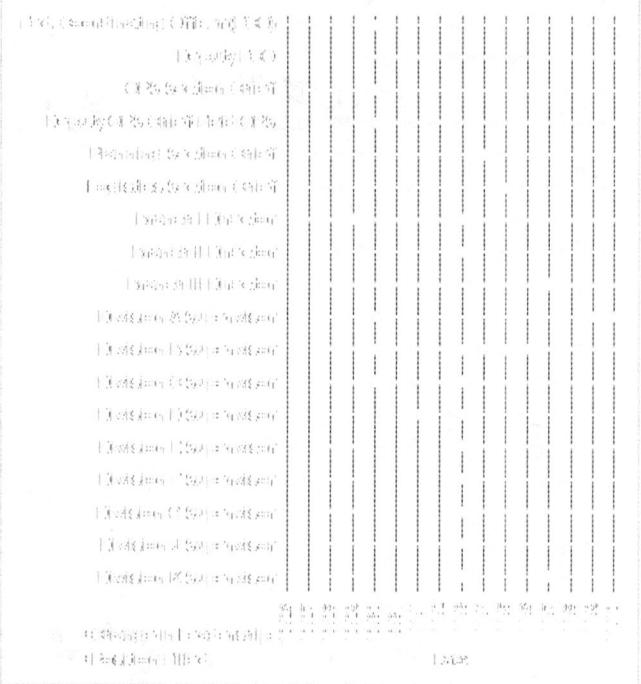

Figure 9: Staffing of leadership positions at the New York JFO changed continuously during the initial two weeks of the response.

center that FEMA operates that serves as the focal point for regional resource coordination. RRCCs are designed to support incident resource coordination until a field operation is established. FEMA guidance, specifically, the 2012-2013 *Operational Guidance and Metrics Memo*, calls upon FEMA to "transition operational control from the Region to the IMAT/FCO within 72 hours of declaration."

At times, Sandy operations created tensions between field and regional staff. For example, transitioning operational control from the Region to the FCO involves delegating Disaster Recovery Manager (DRM) authority, which determines responsibility for managing FEMA programs. During Sandy, FEMA regional and field leadership disagreed over when to transition DRM authority. In addition, field personnel reported that the Region II RRCC, which was supporting operations in New York and New Jersey, struggled to process mission assignments and resource requests as quickly or effectively as needed.

In order to address these challenges, FEMA Headquarters leadership transitioned RRCC functions for New York and New Jersey to the NRCC in Washington, DC. Accordingly, the Region II RRCC transitioned from full Level 1 activation on November 2 to a partial Level 3 activation on November 3. Headquarters leadership believed that this transition of RRCC responsibilities would also facilitate efforts to deploy regional personnel to the field quickly and directly support affected communities.

This transition of RRCC responsibilities caused confusion among some staff, particularly ESF staff supporting the RRCC through mission assignments. These ESF personnel were unclear whether they should await instructions from their home agency or from FEMA. Moreover, Region I—which was supporting Region II activities—reported confusion on how to best offer assistance when the Region II RRCC stood down. Sandy demonstrated that large-scale disasters may affect the traditional role of RRCCs.

Roles and responsibilities of the Area Coordination Group

In an effort to clarify and centralize lines of authority during the Sandy response, FEMA established an Area Coordination Group for Federal Operations in New York and New Jersey on November 2, designating a Deputy Administrator as the Area Coordinator. Under the Area Coordination Group structure, the FCOs for New York and New Jersey retained their authorities and duties but were to report to the Area Coordinator for issues within his purview and to address any other requests directly to the NRCC. As the Area Coordinator, the Deputy Administrator's responsibilities included developing, coordinating, and deconflicting incident objectives, allocating resources based on evolving priorities, ensuring effective incident management and communications, identifying and reporting critical resource needs, and ensuring effective transition to recovery operations.

The Deputy Administrator deployed with a small group of Federal Government personnel and performed Area Coordination duties from a MERS vehicle, allowing them to quickly move throughout the affected area. During his deployment, the Deputy Administrator met with many senior state and local officials, which allowed the FCOs to concentrate on operations. In addition, the Deputy Administrator provided situational awareness to senior leadership in Washington, DC and ensured that the NRCC addressed priorities generated in the field.

Despite these successes, the Area Coordination Group structure and Area Coordinator responsibilities were unfamiliar concepts across the Federal Government and among state and local officials. In particular, Federal partners reported some confusion regarding who had the authority to receive and adjudicate resource requests.

Area for Improvement: Using planning and analysis to drive operational decision-making

FEMA's *Incident Management and Support Keystone* states, "Planning guides incident response and recovery operations at all levels and ensures that the focus remains on achieving incident objectives." At the NRCC, FEMA planners had success adapting deliberate plans to develop a National Support Plan (NSP), which FEMA actively tracked, evaluated, and reported on. More broadly, FEMA experienced challenges in using the planning function to guide operations.

Planning definitions
Deliberate planning is conducted under nonemergency conditions to prepare for known or perceived risks arising from natural hazards or man-made threats.
Crisis action planning is time-sensitive planning conducted in response to a specific, imminent threat or to an incident that has already occurred.

Outside of the NRCC, FEMA struggled to effectively use "deliberate planning" developed pre-incident to then guide "incident planning" during Sandy (see planning definitions in the box above). For example, a survey of FEMA's deployed planners found that 64 percent either never used, nor had access to, regional hurricane plans, which serve as critical pre-incident planning products.

In addition, planners reported that the different planning elements in the NRCC, RRCCs, JFOs, and Initial Operating Facilities (IOFs) worked independently of each other and lacked mechanisms to fully engage Whole Community partners in incident planning. These challenges limited the ability of planning efforts to support operational decision-making. Planners also indicated that they were unclear as to what planning products senior-level decision-makers desired. When planners were assigned to develop ad hoc plans, they sometimes lacked access to the necessary subject-matter expertise. Consequently, planning products did not always meet the needs of operational decision-makers. Conversely, planners were frustrated that leaders were not involved enough in the planning process to ensure that planning efforts reflected leadership guidance.

While many planning challenges arose, there were examples of successful planning efforts. In Nassau County, New York, Federal and state officials worked with the county to jointly develop an Incident Action Plan, demonstrating close integration among key governmental partners in the early hours and days of the operation. As FEMA worked to establish the STEP program (described above), FEMA's team used the planning process outlined in *Comprehensive Preparedness Guide 101*, facilitating coordination among Federal, state, and local officials.

Throughout Sandy response and recovery operations, FEMA also struggled to use analysis to inform outcome-based decision-making. For example, the Office of Response and Recovery (ORR) collected and analyzed data according to its memorandum 2012-2013 *Operational Guidance and Metrics*. This document outlines a detailed set of metrics that ORR uses to assess operational performance. However, the supporting metrics primarily measure outputs (what was done) or efficiency (how quickly something was accomplished), rather than survivor outcomes (e.g., lives saved, lifelines restored). More broadly, Sandy demonstrated FEMA's challenges in collecting and analyzing outcome-based data for a particular disaster, and across multiple disasters. For example, FEMA struggled to analyze power-restoration data from previous disasters in order to assess the effectiveness of Sandy-related power-restoration interventions.

Area for Improvement: Ensuring continuous improvement of disaster doctrine, policies, and plans

Sandy highlighted a number of response and recovery challenges for FEMA and its Whole Community partners. FEMA had previously identified some of these challenges during planning, training, exercise, and operational activities. As one specific example, FEMA's Joplin, Missouri, tornado after-action report identified challenges in using information collection and analysis to drive decision-making—a challenge that emerged again during Sandy. As another example, FEMA does not regularly track whether the Agency addresses capability gaps identified in deliberate planning. Additionally, beyond the NRCC's tracking of *Federal Interagency Response Plan—Hurricane*, FEMA did not document which deliberate plans it used during Sandy, impeding post-incident review and assessment. While the NRCC has a dedicated Lessons Learned Advisor role to support NRCC-level lessons learned and continuous improvement activities, no standardized capability exists for regional or field establishments. Personnel recognized the value of continuous improvement efforts but lacked consistent processes—formal or informal—for documenting and sharing lessons learned and best practices during Sandy field operations. However, FEMA did deploy an ad hoc team from its headquarters to support the collection and analysis of lessons learned in the field.

Together, these examples highlight that, until recently, FEMA lacked a formal, routine process to track and resolve continuous improvement actions across the Agency.FEMA's Lessons Learned/Continuous Improvement Program (LL/CIP) is aimed at addressing this challenge by outlining common processes, tools, and functions for documenting and sharing lessons learned throughout the Agency. As part of the LL/CIP, FEMA has established a FEMA Continuous Improvement Working Group (CIWG), responsible for assigning and tracking continuous improvement actions that are beyond the resolution capability of a single FEMA component or that have Agency-wide implications. The FEMA CIWG includes senior-level representation from FEMA components and will meet at least quarterly. The FEMA CIWG convened its first meeting on February 7, 2013, and will monitor and report on the progress of FEMA components in addressing the areas for improvement identified in this report.

Being Survivor-Centric

Responding to and recovering from disasters is ultimately about meeting survivors' needs. As FEMA states in *Publication 1*, the Agency's "primary responsibility is to support state, local, and tribal partners in caring for all those affected by disaster, and to conduct this support with patience, understanding, and respect." Additionally on November 10, 2012, Administrator Fugate stated to his leadership team, "We must continue to communicate our focus on the needs of the survivors. We must not allow ourselves to define success by the implementation of our programs, nor should we make the survivors fit our process."

In the wake of Sandy, FEMA used new approaches and expedited assistance to meet survivors' housing needs. Leadership at FEMA adopted a posture of "get to yes" to serve survivors and communities. The Agency established a large field presence of more than 1,700 personnel in the Community Relations-Assess, Inform, Report (CR-AIR) function, who served as many survivors' first interaction with FEMA. The Agency also deployed an Innovation Team—a multi-sector, cross-functional group made up of people from various backgrounds, including nonprofit and international organizations, volunteer groups, businesses, and government, as well as concerned community members—to creatively solve problems for survivors.[4]

While these efforts eased the recovery process for a large number of affected individuals, opportunities remain to streamline processes to better serve survivors' needs.

Strength: Meeting survivor needs through innovation

In response to Sandy's widespread effects, FEMA developed new programs and expedited the disbursement of assistance to help survivors find shelter, repair their homes, and receive aid and insurance payments more quickly. FEMA also established a number of initiatives to broaden engagement with survivors and affected communities. These innovations simplified processes for survivors in ways that exemplify FEMA's commitment to providing disaster support and enhancing survivor outcomes.

Sheltering and Temporary Essential Power (STEP) program

At the request of local and state officials, FEMA developed the STEP program to help survivors affected by Sandy in New Jersey, New York, and Connecticut quickly return to or remain in their homes safely (although available, STEP was not implemented in Connecticut). Upon New York and New Jersey's requests, STEP assisted localities in implementing a program to provide the following services:

- *Residential Electrical Meter Repairs* – To accelerate power restoration to residences with storm-damaged electrical meters when broken meters prevent power companies from restoring electricity.

- *Shelter-Essential Measures* – To provide electricity, heat, and hot water to disaster-impacted residences to meet basic life-sustaining needs so that occupants may shelter-in-place until more permanent repairs can be made.

- *Rapid Temporary Exterior Repairs* – To protect storm-damaged residences from further damage that may present an immediate threat to life and property, and to facilitate sheltering-in-place pending permanent repairs. This may include repairs made to accessibility features of a home so that individuals with disabilities are able to access their homes independently.

These services kept survivors in their own homes and sped up their return to normalcy after the disaster. As of February 19, 2013, the STEP program completed more than 18,700 repairs in New York.

---

[4] The Innovation Team's accomplishments are addressed in the next theme, Fostering Unity of Effort Across the Whole Community.

Case Study: Displaced Sandy survivors find free temporary housing through social media rental site

To support temporary housing efforts, New York City partnered with Airbnb, a housing web service that connects people who seek to rent out available living space with those who need a place to stay. In the week following the storm, more than 2,500 reservations were made through the service, representing 4,000 individuals who located temporary housing. In response, Airbnb waived the usual booking fees for hosts and renters and provided the standard insurance protection for rentals. Subsequently, more than 1,400 Airbnb users signed up to offer their homes at no cost, providing free, temporary housing to those in need.

Neighborhood Task Force Initiative

To meet the unique needs and diverse cultures of New York City neighborhoods, the New York JFO created the Neighborhood Task Force Initiative. The Task Force assigned a Neighborhood Crew— composed of Community Relations representatives, a Disability Integration Advisor (DIA), a Voluntary Agency Liaison, FEMA Corps members, and Public and Individual Assistance representatives—to the hardest hit neighborhoods. Members of the Task Force remained in place for 60 days and supported communities by fixing problems and simplifying bureaucratic processes.

Support, Execute, Record, Verify, and Evaluate (SERVE) program

The New York JFO implemented the SERVE program to immediately resolve survivor concerns raised during town hall meetings and community events. Community Relations and Individual Assistance teams were able to mitigate survivor distress by accessing Federal disaster aid applications on the spot. SERVE reached over 5,000 people at approximately 55 town hall meetings.

Case Study: Power and shelter relief services provided through Proctor & Gamble partnership

Building on a partnership and lessons learned from Hurricanes Katrina and Isaac, the Proctor & Gamble emergency response teams, the American Red Cross, and the Tide® Loads of Hope™ responders joined forces to provide services to families and individuals. In addition to providing showers, personal care kits, household products, baby products, and a free laundry service, the team established a Duracell Power Forward Center in Battery Park, New York, and deployed a Rapid Responder 4x4 truck into the affected streets of New York and New Jersey. The power center and Rapid Responder vehicle distributed free batteries, provided cell phone and laptop recharging services, and offered Wi-Fi internet access. In the three weeks following the storm, the Power Forward initiative provided over 125,000 batteries, charged more than 1,000 cell phones, and helped more than 10,000 families affected by Sandy.

"Check Your Home" tool

To provide information to survivors whose homes were in restricted access areas, especially on the New Jersey barrier islands, FEMA developed and released the "Check Your Home" mobile application and web portal. The tool allowed users to enter their addresses and view aerial imagery of the storm's effects on their homes. The New Jersey Office of Emergency Management highlighted the Check Your Home tool, shown in Figure 10, via social media. Several publications and internet sites praised the service and noted its value to survivors who might otherwise have no information on the status of their homes.

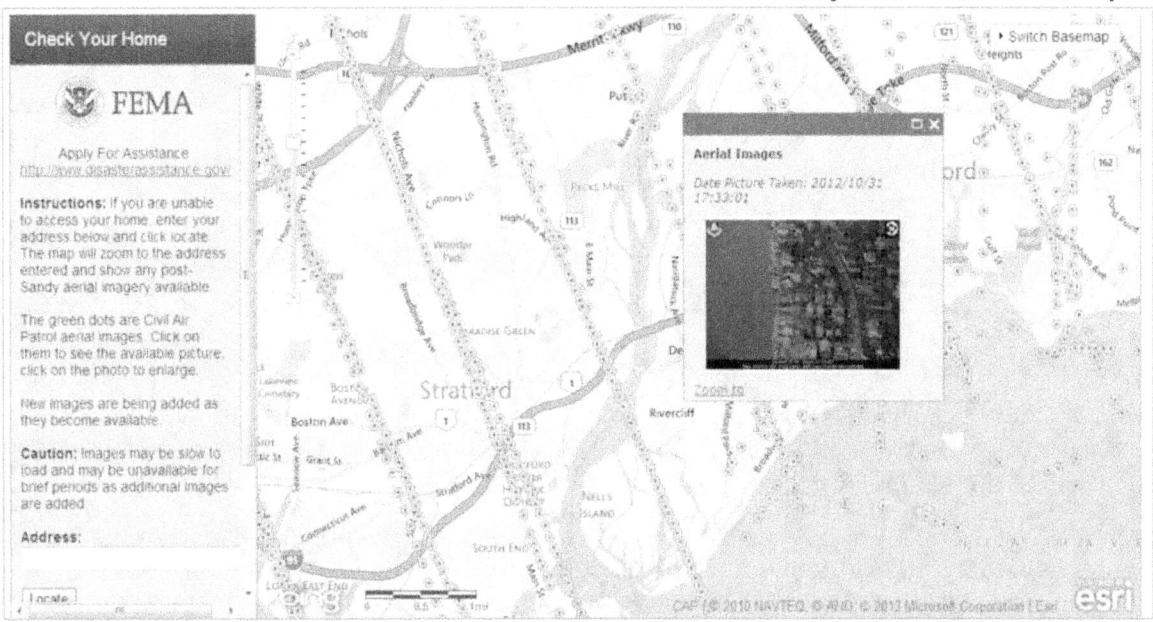

Figure 10: FEMA's "Check Your Home" application allowed survivors whose homes were in restricted areas to view aerial images of them.

Rental assistance

In the days following Sandy's landfall, FEMA evaluated the number of rental resources within metropolitan New York and northern New Jersey that might be available to house disaster survivors. To account for the high rental costs in the region, FEMA authorized funds to increase the existing rental assistance in New York and New Jersey to 125 percent of the current Fiscal Year 2013 levels. The Agency also used the results of geospatial analysis by its Modeling Task Force (MOTF) to offer expedited rental assistance to survivors who could not access their homes. The MOTF analyzed information from a number of data sources—including high watermark sensors, inundation levels, imagery data from the National Oceanic and Atmospheric Administration, and road closure information from states' Departments of Transportation—to develop a list of communities that housing inspectors would be unlikely to access for days or weeks. Households in locations that the MOTF models showed to be inaccessible automatically qualified for two months of rental assistance at the increased rate. This non-traditional approach to meeting survivor needs contributed to 44,000 households receiving expedited rental assistance.

National Flood Insurance Program

Sandy brought a record storm surge for the area that inundated the New Jersey coast, lower Manhattan, the Rockaway Peninsula in Queens, and large sections of southern Staten Island. The resultant flooding destroyed thousands of homes. To help communities recover more quickly, FEMA's National Flood Insurance Program (NFIP) adapted to support survivors. In particular, ahead of adjuster inspections, the Program authorized partial payments of up to $30,000 to cover building system and related repairs when prompt action was necessary to preserve health and safety. The Program also extended the timeframe in which an insured survivor could submit a proof of loss, from 60 days to one year from that loss. Finally, the NFIP instituted a rapid claims process that resulted in some policyholders receiving up to $5,000 against their coverage for the building contents, pending final settlement of their claims. Advance payments for this and other items constituted roughly $1.2 billion of the $4.8 billion that the NFIP paid for Sandy-associated claims through February 20, 2013.

Case Study: Fast-thinking officials rally community resources to reunite pets with owners

Many anxious pet owners placed themselves in harm's way when attempting to reunite with pets left behind in areas ravaged by the storm. The New Jersey Governor's Office of Emergency Management worked with representatives from the New Jersey Department of Agriculture, the U.S. Department of Agriculture, and the Humane Society of the United States to establish an emergency hotline and coordinate pet-recovery efforts. Tapping into well-established telecommunication systems and community resources, the team coordinated with and engaged local responders, volunteers, and nonprofits to search for, recover, care for, and reunite more than 400 pets with their owners.

Area for Improvement: Meeting survivors' needs during initial interactions

FEMA historically has separated the functions of its Community Relations and Applicant Services personnel. Community Relations personnel are trained to provide survivors with an overview of available assistance programs and explanations of how to register. Applicant Services personnel are trained to assist with registration, check the status of an application, and explain the next steps. Additionally, Applicant Services personnel have traditionally been positioned at stationary DRCs and shelters, while Community Relations teams have been located in neighborhoods, meeting survivors at their homes. FEMA made strides combining these functions to bring registration assistance directly to survivors, but opportunities remain to make programs easier for survivors to access.

Community Relations—Assess, Inform, Report (CR–AIR)

In response to Sandy, FEMA deployed over 1,700 Community Relations Specialists to establish a large presence in affected communities. However, the mission faced challenges caused by inexperienced staff and insufficient management, which, in turn, were magnified by the sheer volume of deployed personnel.

To meet the staffing need, many CR-AIR personnel who deployed had only taken a three-hour training course. More than 70 percent of personnel assigned to CR-AIR were new to the assignment, and half had no prior

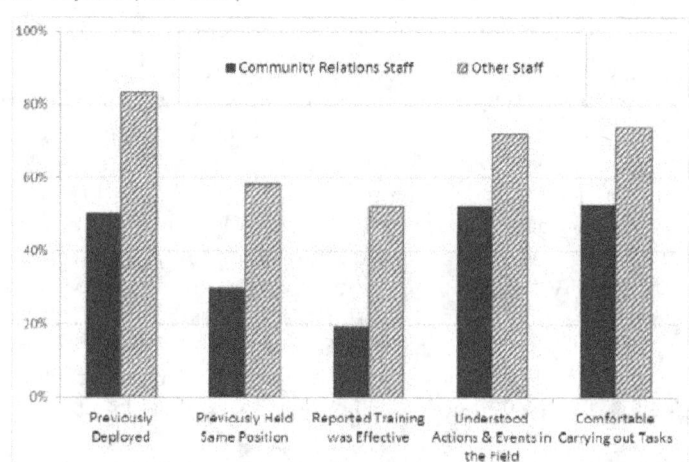

Figure 11: CR–AIR staff reported being less experienced, under-prepared, and less comfortable carrying out their assignments than other FEMA personnel that deployed in response to Sandy.

disaster experience. Figure 11 illustrates the relative inexperience and insufficient training of the CR-AIR staff, along with the resulting lack of confidence in their abilities to perform their assignments. In some cases, inexperienced Community Relations Specialists were unprepared to answer survivors' questions about FEMA's programs.

The CR-AIR mission also suffered from a lack of management and clear objectives from field operations supervisors. While the CR-AIR cadre contains a staff of experienced managers, confusion regarding new procedures for requesting staff resulted in FEMA deploying managers as lower-level specialists and assigning personnel to leadership roles on an ad hoc basis. In addition, the CR-AIR mission experienced uneven coordination with Division Supervisors. Division Supervisors were not always aware of JFO decisions to send CR-AIR teams to their assigned geographic location. Personnel management was further complicated by confusion about when the CR-AIR mission was considered complete. The large number of CR-AIR personnel in the field allowed teams to cover ground relatively quickly. However, CR-AIR leadership had limited ability to track which areas teams had already covered. Consequently, CR-AIR teams visited several areas multiple times, frustrating residents who were eager to receive services. Additionally, survivors asked CR-AIR personnel to answer questions regarding their Individual Assistance cases, which not all CR-AIR personnel could answer.

Lastly, the CR-AIR staff struggled to provide leadership with clear and actionable data based on field observations. The mechanisms for CR-AIR teams to report information were time-consuming and unstandardized. Moreover, some CR-AIR staff did not use the mobile application designed to streamline this process because they lacked tablets.

Together, these challenges decreased the effectiveness of some of FEMA's initial interactions with survivors. FEMA's recent action to transfer CR-AIR functions from the Office of External Affairs to the Recovery Directorate is aimed at expanding the services provided during FEMA's first interactions with disaster survivors.

Case Study: Teams bring FEMA registration directly to survivors

FEMA Corps and Surge Capacity Teams supporting CR-AIR used tablet devices to complete roving disaster assistance registrations and answer questions related to disaster survivor cases for communities affected by Sandy. In one example, FEMA brought the registration process directly to survivors on Staten Island, providing needed assistance without having to visit a DRC or place a phone call. While the scope of this effort on Staten Island was comparatively small (it registered 116 survivors), it eased the burden on survivors in one of the hardest-hit areas.

Disaster Recovery Centers

DRCs are facilities or mobile offices where survivors may go to get information about and register for disaster assistance programs. While DRCs registered a large number of people for disaster assistance, DRC processes were not oriented to efficiently meet survivor needs. The process of seeking assistance at a DRC often required survivors to repeat information to multiple individuals, lengthening the overall process.

In addition, DRCs were not consistent in the services they provided to survivors, and these differences were not necessarily related to customized needs of the local community. For example, some DRCs included local nonprofits, banking, or insurance representatives, while others were limited to information on Federal programs. Some DRCs included charging stations for phones and electronic devices and had disaster assistance registration kiosks.

Call centers

FEMA also serves disaster survivors through its three National Processing Service Center (NPSC) call centers. Survivors use these call centers to register for disaster assistance and to receive information about the services FEMA provides. Although the call centers processed over half a million applications following Sandy, they did not have the staff or technology needed to keep pace with survivors' requests

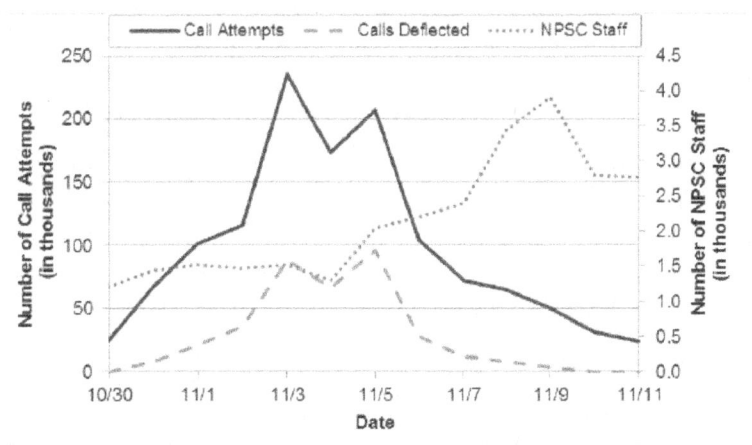

Figure 12: FEMA did not surge call center staff to peak levels until well after call volume had peaked.

for information. In the earliest phases of the response, daily call volume peaked on November 3, with more than 235,000 call attempts (see Figure 12). However, approximately 38 percent of these calls were deflected, in which case survivors received a pre-recorded message to visit the website *www.disasterassistance.gov*, or to call back at another time. While additional call center support staff from the

Internal Revenue Service augmented NPSC staff capabilities, this assistance did not reach its maximum levels until November 9, almost a week after call volume had already peaked.

In addition, technological limitations further affected NPSC call center effectiveness. For example, the call-routing system is not capable of offering automated status updates to callers about their applications, meaning that individuals must speak to a representative each time they call.

Area for Improvement: Ensuring all survivors have equal access to services

FEMA is committed to assisting survivors with disabilities and others who have access and functional needs. As part of Sandy response and recovery efforts, FEMA deployed RDISs, Equal Rights Advisors, and newly created DIAs to advise field leadership and ensure that all survivor needs were considered and integrated into operations.

The DIA position is a recent addition to FEMA's deployable workforce; the process to create the position began in May of 2012. As FQS implementation is still ongoing, FEMA has not yet officially qualified personnel in DIA positions. In order to fill DIA positions during Sandy, FEMA deployed surge staff from its Office of Disability Integration and Coordination, and used mission assignments to deploy additional non-FEMA disability specialists to augment DIA capabilities. Several DIAs developed innovative approaches to assisting survivors with access and functional needs. For example, the DIA in the New York JFO established a system to assist Individual Assistance and CR-AIR identify, track, and address the immediate needs of survivors with disabilities and access and functional needs. The system, which was also used by FEMA's Voluntary Agency Liaison, helped the Agency connect survivors with community-based resources.

Individuals serving in DIA roles focused on divergent aspects of their mission during Sandy. For example, different DIAs focused on assisting with lifesaving and life-sustaining efforts, facilitating equal access to communications, engaging community partners, training Federal personnel to communicate with individuals with access and functional needs, and ensuring access to equipment to support equal access to effective communication at FEMA DRCs. In addition to their divergent focus areas, DIAs reported that JFO staff and other deployed personnel were unsure of DIA functions and roles. After-action efforts further revealed confusion regarding FEMA's role in the immediate lifesaving and life-sustaining needs of individuals with access and functional needs—such as the Agency's legal responsibility to safeguard personal information—and in ensuring equal access to and inclusion in all aspects of response and recovery programs and activities. These divergent DIA focus areas and associated challenges highlighted the need for greater clarity and training on the role of DIAs—both for those serving in that role and for those who interact with DIAs. FEMA has already taken steps to address this challenge, outlining the responsibilities of the DIA role in its updated January 2013 *Incident Management Handbook* (IMH) and is currently completing a training course for JFO and field staff.

Area for Improvement: Reducing the complexity of the Public Assistance program

FEMA's PA program helps communities address the impact of Sandy, particularly the millions of cubic yards of debris across the East Coast that the storm generated, as well as the hundreds of millions of dollars in damages to government-owned facilities. The PA program provides funding for debris removal; emergency protective measures; and the repair, replacement, or restoration of disaster-damaged, publicly owned facilities, as well as the facilities of certain private nonprofit organizations. The Agency implemented several new initiatives that streamlined the program for eligible applicants, but Sandy nonetheless revealed challenges with PA implementation.

Figure 13: Hurricane Sandy brought a stranded tanker ship to shore in Staten Island, NY.

During Sandy, FEMA published a new rule for debris-removal work performed under the Stafford Act Major Disaster or Emergency Assistance Programs, which allows jurisdictions to be reimbursed for permanent employees' salaries and benefits. These provisions will provide an incentive to jurisdictions to focus the regular workforce—as opposed to contract labor—on removing Sandy-related debris, contributing to a quicker and more efficient recovery.

FEMA also took several steps to help government officials better understand the PA program and to reduce the complexity of program rules. These steps included:

- Deploying senior Agency leadership to provide policy interpretation and guidance;

- Initiating the hiring of Cadre of On-Call Response/Recovery Employees (CORE) for two-year, excepted-service positions to perform and manage Sandy-related PA projects; and

- Releasing a draft decision memorandum explaining the rules for PA project determinations to serve as guidance for state, local, and tribal officials.

Case Study: FEMA's Public Assistance program helps New York University medical center rebuild

In order to accelerate recovery efforts in New York City, FEMA engaged potential PA applicants responsible for the restoration of critical functions—such as hospitals and police stations—early in the response. For example, FEMA convened within one week of landfall a conference call with area hospitals to explain the program and the application process. The FEMA Administrator subsequently met with senior leaders from several hospitals, including officials from New York University (NYU) Langone Medical Center.

FEMA, NYU, and New York State worked together to expeditiously complete a PA Project Worksheet for the medical center in early November. As a result of this collaboration, FEMA has obligated more than $114 million to the NYU Medical Langone Medical Center for patient evacuation, emergency repairs, and clean-up of critical services and facilities. The NYU award demonstrates FEMA's commitment to ensuring that local governments and private nonprofits obtain as quickly as possible the maximum disaster assistance they are eligible for under the law.

Despite these steps to improve program consistency, state and local officials in New York and New Jersey have continued to express confusion regarding PA efforts. Specific frustrations include turnover in PA points of contact and requirements/rules governing the project-approval process.

A lack of clarity regarding the scope of the program has also delayed recovery efforts. Several coastal communities, for instance, are waiting to clean up offshore debris (such as abandoned vessels) until they receive a definitive answer on whether such an expense would be reimbursed. Local officials are also concerned that the slow pace of reimbursement will cripple their local budgets.

The Sandy Recovery Improvement Act of 2013 provides FEMA alternative procedures to approve PA projects. These procedures are intended to:

- Reduce the costs to the Federal Government of providing PA;

- Increase flexibility in the administration of PA;

- Expedite the provision of such assistance to a state, tribal, or local government, or to an owner or operator of a private nonprofit facility; and

- Provide financial incentives and disincentives for a state, tribal, or local government, or for an owner or operator of a private nonprofit facility for the timely and cost-effective completion of projects receiving such assistance.

These new PA procedures can serve as a springboard for FEMA to continue reducing the complexity of the PA program so that it more effectively helps communities recover from disasters. FEMA is currently developing specific implementation procedures for the new PA authority granted under the Sandy Recovery Improvement Act. These implementation procedures will detail the applicability of each PA provision, provide further guidance as to how the authority will be implemented, and may include metrics and other assessment tools and procedures.

Fostering Unity of Effort Across the Whole Community

FEMA's response and recovery operations can be effective only if they are implemented in concert with the activities of the Whole Community—including all levels of government, private and nonprofit sectors, faith-based organizations, communities, and individuals.

In recent years, FEMA has consistently stressed the importance of integrating with a wide variety of partners, especially those from outside government. This Whole Community approach looks beyond government-centric disaster management and focuses on creating unified disaster response and recovery efforts that leverage the capabilities of the entire Nation. Sandy demonstrated that FEMA has made progress in realizing this vision. The storm also revealed opportunities for FEMA to further improve coordination with Whole Community members. As the Agency looks to prepare for the full range of potential disasters, FEMA recognizes that it must work together with all community members before incidents occur and effectively coordinate with Whole Community partners during incident response and recovery.

Strength: Integrating response efforts with nongovernmental partners

During Sandy, FEMA demonstrated progress in integrating its response and recovery efforts with the Whole Community by deploying an Innovation Team and coordinating with private, faith-based, nongovernmental organizations. In addition, FEMA leveraged the capacity of private individuals by crowd-sourcing information.

Case Study: Veteran-focused disaster response team rallies to aid recovery efforts

Team Rubicon is a nongovernmental organization composed of first responders, medical professionals, and military veterans who deploy to global disaster zones. Formed in response to the 2010 Haiti earthquake, the organization employs the talents and skills of veterans to provide high-impact public service support.

Following Sandy, Team Rubicon organized and deployed more than 300 military and 5,000 civilian volunteers to support recovery efforts in Far Rockaway, New York, constituting its largest operation to date. Team Rubicon volunteers, in collaboration with New York City's Office of Emergency Management, established an operations base in a gated parking lot, where they organized volunteers, processed work orders, and tracked operations using logistics programs and geospatial software. Within six days of activation, Team Rubicon volunteers rescued people trapped in floodwaters, delivered thousands of pounds of emergency supplies, tended to the medical needs of hundreds of evacuees, and supported residential clean-up efforts.

Innovation Team

On November 2, FEMA deployed an Innovation Team—a multi-sector, cross-functional group made up of people from various backgrounds, including nonprofit and international organizations, volunteer groups, businesses, and government, as well as concerned community members. FEMA asked the Innovation Team to creatively solve problems for survivors. Working from a New York City field office, the team identified challenges and developed a number of solutions, including:

- Deploying Very Small Aperture Terminal satellite communications equipment, providing internet access for field personnel and survivors, reducing the need for FEMA to deploy Mobile Command Operating Vehicles;

- Working with the private sector and FEMA field leadership to set up Voice over Internet Protocol telephone systems, wireless networks, and high-throughput satellite terminals, in order to provide nongovernmental organizations, volunteers, community organizations, and survivors with Internet access;

- Arranging for Polish and Russian translators for unexpected medical and response support requirements within a community severely affected by the storm;

- Arranging for the reproduction of hard-copy maps to support responders and volunteers unfamiliar with local geography;

- Identifying local multi-lingual radio and newspaper mass media channels and passing that information to non-local responders for community messaging;

- Identifying and addressing DRC design shortfalls that caused visible confusion for disaster survivors; and

- Debunking rumors and misinformation by investigating their origin and getting accurate information out to the public through social media.

The diverse backgrounds of Innovation Team members contributed to the solutions they developed. The Innovation Team consistently demonstrated a "get to yes" mindset and showed FEMA's commitment to working with Whole Community partners to address challenges confronting disaster survivors.

National Business Emergency Operations Center (NBEOC)

The NBEOC is a virtual organization established in 2011 that serves as a clearinghouse for two-way information sharing between public- and private sector stakeholders in preparing for, responding to, and recovering from disasters. During Sandy, the NBEOC provided situational awareness to the private sector, responded to private sector inquiries, and identified and resolved critical private sector needs and issues.

With its communications and coordinating facilities housed in the NRCC, the NBEOC also directly benefited survivors and responders by channeling critical information and resources from a number of private sector companies to affected communities. For example, the American Hotel and Lodging Association reached out to its membership to promote the TSA program. This outreach helped to increase the available housing resources for disaster survivors and emergency personnel in New York and New Jersey. The NBEOC garnered significant participation from the private sector but some government and private sector partners were unclear about the distinction between NBEOC functions and the responsibilities of the National Infrastructure Coordinating Center. In addition, NBEOC disseminated situational reports only to their members, which limited FEMA's ability to directly connect with businesses in the affected areas. These challenges demonstrate the need to further define and clarify NBEOC roles and responsibilities.

Case Study: Solar Sandy project reconnects communities devastated by Sandy

Solar power companies in New York and New Jersey partnered to deploy equipment and volunteers to install and maintain mobile solar power generators in some of the hardest-hit communities. Solar One, SolarCity, Consolidated Solar, and the New York State Energy Research and Development Authority dispatched teams of volunteers with 10-kilowatt mobile solar generators to provide much-needed temporary electricity to multiple locations in the Rockaways, on Staten Island, and in New Jersey. The solar power systems allowed survivors and relief workers to charge cell phones, power laptops, heat food, and power other critical electronic equipment.

Faith-based organizations

Ensuring that FEMA connects to faith leaders and communities is important for reaching disaster survivors and for leveraging resources from faith-based organizations to support those in need. Sandy's impact prompted FEMA to coordinate with the DHS Center of Faith-based and Neighborhood Partnerships to undertake several new efforts to engage faith-based organizations in response and recovery activities. For the first time, staff from the White House Office of Faith-based and Neighborhood Partnerships deployed to the field to support disaster survivors. Specifically, deployed staff focused their efforts on connecting faith leaders with FEMA programs, understanding pockets of urgent need, and inviting leaders to engage FEMA through town halls to address key questions.

Voluntary Organizations Active in Disasters (VOADs)

VOADs provide important services directly to responders and affected communities before, during, and after disasters. VOADs often serve the essential needs of survivors, thereby decreasing the resources that governments must coordinate and supply.

The work of the American Red Cross demonstrates the importance of VOADs. The American Red Cross is the Nation's largest provider of mass care services and a

Figure 14: The American Red Cross sets up at a Disaster Recovery Center.

supporting agency for ESF #6 (Mass Care). The organization was instrumental in Sandy response and recovery efforts. During its peak operations, on October 29, the American Red Cross sheltered 10,928 residents in 258 shelters, accounting for 70 percent of all open shelters. In addition, as of January 28, 2013, the organization had provided over 11 million meals and snacks to survivors. In total, the American Red Cross staffed relief operations with more than 15,800 disaster responders.

Similarly, the Salvation Army performed critical response and recovery efforts. Immediately following Sandy, the Salvation Army began to coordinate the delivery of essential services and resources—including meals, snacks, water, blankets, baby formula, toiletries, batteries, and flashlights—to survivors. The Salvation Army distributed more than 4.6 million meals, snacks, and drinks to Sandy survivors across multiple states. In total, more than 7,500 Salvation Army volunteers logged more than 24,000 hours of service. In addition, Southern Baptist Disaster Relief served almost two million meals and coordinated over 40,000 volunteer days of service.

Crowd-sourcing information

Figure 15: Both FEMA and Google distributed the Humanitarian OpenStreetMap Team's grid map that showed the results of volunteers' damage assessments.

Volunteers from across the country collaborated online to assist survivors in the immediate aftermath of Sandy. For the Humanitarian OpenStreetMap Team's MapMill project, volunteers used aerial imagery from the National Oceanic and Atmospheric Administration and the Civil Air Patrol to assess damages to buildings and infrastructure. Working mostly on November 1-3, over 6,000 volunteers assessed the damage from aerial imagery as light, moderate, or heavy. Volunteers completed over 137,000 assessments of more than 35,000 images. The Humanitarian OpenStreetMap Team then used the results to create a color-coded grid map depicting damages throughout the area (see Figure 15). To expand distribution, Google included the map and images on its Sandy CrisisMap, and FEMA included it on the Agency's internal GeoPortal site. The effort provided a powerful example of the possibilities that crowd-sourcing holds for the future. The challenge for FEMA will be to determine how to further use crowd-sourced information to inform decision-making and disaster assistance programs.

Case Study: High school students innovate to address gas shortages in wake of Sandy

Students at Franklin High School in New Brunswick, New Jersey used the online mapping service, Mappler, to publish information on whether gas stations in the area were open, had power, had available fuel, and/or served as charging stations. Students gathered information from personal observations, direct contact with gas stations, media reports, and updates from social media outlets such as Twitter and Facebook. The students created a map outlining the status of fuel resources in the community. The information then fed directly into Google's Crisis Map, allowing thousands of people to access the information. This current information significantly reduced the wait times for drivers seeking to refuel and assisted the efforts of FEMA and other government and commercial partners in directing power and fuel resources to the areas most affected by the storm.

Case Study: Smartphone apps provide critical information to Sandy responders and survivors

Several organizations, including the American Red Cross, the U.S. Department of Veterans Affairs (VA), and FEMA have developed smartphone applications designed for rapid dissemination to survivors and disaster workers. Among the various applications used during Sandy were the American Red Cross's Hurricane app, the VA's Psychological First Aid (PFA) app, and FEMA's Emergency Preparedness app. Over 100,000 users downloaded the American Red Cross's Hurricane app to monitor and track the storm, prepare for the disaster, and locate shelters. The VA's PFA app—downloaded more than 1,800 times—provides guidance on administering psychological first aid to adults, families, and children. The FEMA Emergency Preparedness app—downloaded by more than 50,000 users—provides an interactive checklist for emergency kits, maps with disaster recovery and shelter information, and an online application for assistance. Despite widespread power and cell phone outages, the use of smartphone applications provided necessary information to both survivors and responders.

Area for Improvement: Coordinating among states, localities, and tribes

As defined in the NRF, the Unified Coordination Group (UCG) is the primary construct for coordinating state and Federal activities at the JFO. This group comprises "senior leaders representing Federal and state interests (the FCO and the State Coordinating Officer) and, in certain circumstances, tribal governments, local jurisdictions, and the private sector." According to FEMA's IMH, the FCO and State Coordinating Officer jointly decide membership of the UCG.

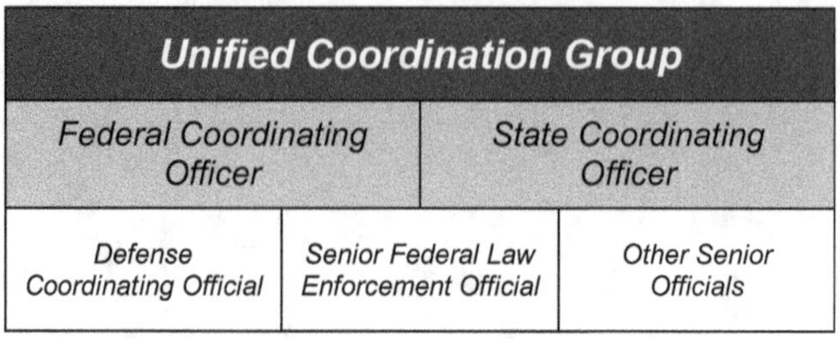

Unified Coordination Group		
Federal Coordinating Officer		State Coordinating Officer
Defense Coordinating Official	Senior Federal Law Enforcement Official	Other Senior Officials

Figure 16: UCG doctrine was in effect during Sandy.

FEMA coordinates with states, which in turn support coordination with localities and tribes. As discussed above, FEMA's combined organization approach—with geographic Branch Directors and Division Supervisors—provided direct linkages to local community needs and perspectives during Sandy. However, the scope of Sandy and its impacts on densely populated localities (particularly New York City) presented challenges for FEMA. The city and state did not jointly develop resource requests or priorities before providing them to the Federal Government. In one case, New York City and New York State officials gave conflicting directions to USACE regarding tunnel pumping, causing confusion regarding pumping priorities. To address these challenges, FEMA's January 2013 IMH emphasizes the potential for local officials to be included in UCGs, in order to more rapidly address requirements in coordination with the state.

For tribal integration, Sandy was the first NRCC activation to include a tribal affairs liaison. The position in the NRCC was filled with both FEMA and Bureau of Indian Affairs representatives, the latter via mission assignment. For its field operations, FEMA has Tribal Affairs Specialists who are responsible for tribal coordination. When Sandy hit, FEMA had six fully qualified staff and nine trainee staff (per FQS) for these tribal positions. For Sandy, FEMA focused its tribal coordination efforts on the Shinnecock Indian Nation, located in New York, through a Tribal Affairs Specialist who arranged Community Relations and Applicant Specialist visits, in addition to coordinating PA kickoff meetings.

Moving forward, the Sandy Recovery Improvement Act of 2013, which included an amendment to the Robert T. Stafford Act, acknowledges the sovereignty of federally recognized tribes by allowing them to make emergency and disaster declaration requests directly to the President. Furthermore, FEMA's January 2013 IMH and 2013 *Regional Incident Support Manual* both emphasize the importance of coordinating with tribal nations and account for tribal participation in UCGs. FEMA's Special Advisor for National Tribal Affairs acknowledged the need for broader education across FEMA regarding tribal coordination and the staffing challenges that the Agency will face in scaling up the existing tribal affairs coordination capabilities to ensure effective coordination with the 566 federally recognized tribes.

Case Study: Occupy Sandy tackles disaster response

Occupy Sandy is a grassroots volunteer disaster relief movement which provided innovative support to Sandy recovery efforts. Within four months, Occupy Sandy amassed 60,000 volunteers, collected nearly $1 million in donations for Sandy survivors, and distributed food, clothing, medical supplies, and construction materials. Occupy Sandy impacted thousands of survivors in New York and New Jersey. Some of Occupy Sandy's notable accomplishments included:

- Establishing food distribution centers in Brooklyn and other hubs, such as Coney Island;

- Setting up online donation and volunteer social media sites;

- Serving nearly 10,000 meals a day in the week after Sandy made landfall, through 15,000 volunteers recruited via social media sites; and

- Coordinating motor pools to transport construction teams and medical committees to survivors in the field.

FEMA's Innovation Team worked closely with Occupy Sandy to support survivors and develop solutions to challenges in the affected areas.

Developing an Agile, Professional Emergency Management Workforce

In announcing the 2012 initiative to transform FEMA's workforce into a more professional, deployable organization—"Every Employee an Emergency Manager"—FEMA Deputy Administrator Serino reminded Agency staff that "FEMA's fundamental goal, and the inspiration and motivation for many FEMA employees, is to serve the nation by helping its people and first responders, especially when they are most in need."

FEMA employees have demonstrated their dedication throughout the Agency's history, and they did so again during Sandy. Many FEMA staff volunteered to deploy to the affected areas to provide on-the-ground support to survivors. In addition, the Agency completed one of the largest personnel deployments in its history. For this deployment, FEMA not only used traditional deployable resources such as Reservists (formerly Disaster Assistance Employees), but also relied more heavily on its permanent staff and non-FEMA employees (including the DHS SCF and FEMA Corps members). In addition, FEMA's workforce consists of local hires, which numbered almost 700 in New York and New Jersey by February 2013.

The size of the Sandy deployment created challenges for FEMA. Given the in-progress nature of FEMA's disaster workforce transformation, the Agency sent a number of under-trained and under-supported personnel to the field. The orders to deploy a large number of personnel also left several FEMA components without a clear understanding of what level of daily operations Agency leadership expected them to maintain. In some cases, FEMA components were left without the personnel needed to meet expectations that arose in the weeks following Sandy's landfall. FEMA's response to Sandy illustrated that large-scale incidents stretch the Agency's ability to deploy a large workforce capable of meeting response and recovery needs.

Strength: Completing one of the largest and most diverse personnel deployments in FEMA history

In 2011, FEMA established a force structure that estimates the number of personnel the Agency requires in incident management and support roles to respond to multiple major incidents, including those with severe impacts. To meet these force structure requirements—totaling more than 30,000 personnel—FEMA has sought to improve and diversify the mechanisms through which it recruits and retains disaster personnel. These mechanisms include an overhaul of the former Disaster Assistance Employee Program to a new Reservist Program that includes health benefits, the launch of a DHS SCF, and a partnership with the Corporation for National and Community Service on an innovative program called FEMA Corps.

DHS Surge Capacity Force and Sandy support

The Post Katrina Emergency Management Reform Act of 2006 directed DHS to establish an SCF capable of augmenting FEMA's workforce. DHS SCF personnel are trained to support response and recovery operations and are deployable within 48 hours of warning, alert, or no-notice activation. There are currently over 3,800 DHS volunteers signed up to be a part of the SCF.

DHS trains SCF volunteers in logistics, Community Relations, Individual Assistance, and Public Assistance. While the SCF contributed to the response in these key areas, volunteers with in-demand skills were also integrated into other missions, such as Language Teams and Housing Inspections. In some instances, SCF teams were assigned special projects. For example, the Individual Assistance Branch at the New York JFO tasked 130 SCF members to call survivors who self-identified with access and functional needs, confirming their need and providing them with information on vetted resources. Over 19,000 calls were made, identifying more than 3,000 survivors in need of additional assistance.

To meet Sandy's requirements, FEMA drew upon all of these new programs to complete one of the Agency's largest and most diverse deployments of personnel to date. As of December 31, 2012, FEMA had deployed 9,971 personnel to support Sandy response and recovery efforts. Over 900 FEMA personnel pre-deployed before Sandy's landfall on October 29, with the total surging to nearly 8,000 people two weeks later. The number of personnel deployed during Sandy exceeded the total deployed for Hurricanes Isaac (2012) and Irene (2012) combined (see Figure 17).

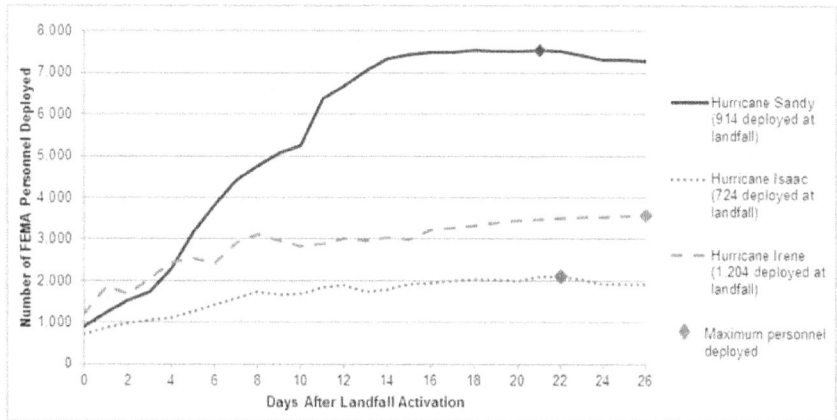

Figure 17: FEMA deployed more people for Sandy response and recovery operations than it did for Hurricanes Isaac and Irene combined, and the Agency reached its peak deployment level more quickly than it did for those incidents.

Furthermore, the response to Sandy demonstrated that FEMA's disaster workforce is beginning to better reflect its force structure goals. For example, 47 percent of the FEMA force structure (excluding DHS SCF) is composed of Reservists—and the FEMA and FEMA Corps workforce responding at Sandy's peak included 60 percent Reservists, as compared to 69 percent at the peak of Hurricane Irene and 78 percent at the peak of Hurricane Isaac.

Moreover, Sandy marked the first mass deployment of FEMA Corps and the historic inaugural activation of the DHS SCF. These groups represented 6 percent and 14 percent of the total workforce, respectively (see Figure 19). FEMA field offices identified staffing requirements and requested FEMA Corps members through FEMA's Incident Workforce Management Division (IWMD).[5] IWMD deployed 42 FEMA Corps teams. FEMA Corps personnel registered survivors for individual assistance, supported the establishment of DRCs, and staffed CR-AIR teams. Sandy was also the first deployment of the DHS SCF, with a total of 1,194 DHS SCF members supporting response and recovery operations in New York and New Jersey. Ultimately, FEMA's efforts to

Figure 18: FEMA Administrator Craig Fugate discusses disaster field operations with a FEMA Corps team in Lincroft, New Jersey.

meet its force structure requirements—through a more robust Reservist Program, increased use of permanent full-time (PFT) staff and CORE, and innovative partnerships such as FEMA Corps and the DHS SCF—contributed to FEMA's ability to execute this large-scale deployment of personnel.

---

[5] FEMA IWMD was previously called the Incident Workforce Management Office (IWMO). Following Hurricane Sandy, FEMA elevated IWMO to the Division-level.

FEMA Corps and Sandy support

In March 2012, FEMA and the Corporation for National and Community Service announced a partnership to establish a FEMA-devoted unit of service corps members solely devoted to disaster preparedness, response, and recovery. The program will prepare up to 1,600 young people each year for future careers in emergency management.

During the Sandy response and recovery efforts, FEMA Corps members played important roles in supporting disaster survivors, including:

- Working directly with survivors on CR-AIR teams in New York and New Jersey to answer questions and register survivors for FEMA assistance;

- Supporting DRC operations, including setting up a mobile DRC in Union Beach;

- Helping survivors find hotel accommodations, running donation centers, and supporting shelter operations;

- Participating in a CR-AIR pilot program using tablet devices to complete roving disaster assistance registrations in Staten Island; and

- Providing translation services to assist survivors who did not speak English register for FEMA assistance.

Area for Improvement: Ensuring a qualified disaster workforce

As of October 1, 2012, FEMA launched a new FQS that defines the training, experience, and demonstrated performance required to become credentialed in each of the disaster workforce positions. In anticipation of that launch, FEMA conducted an initial qualifications review of existing disaster personnel that resulted in

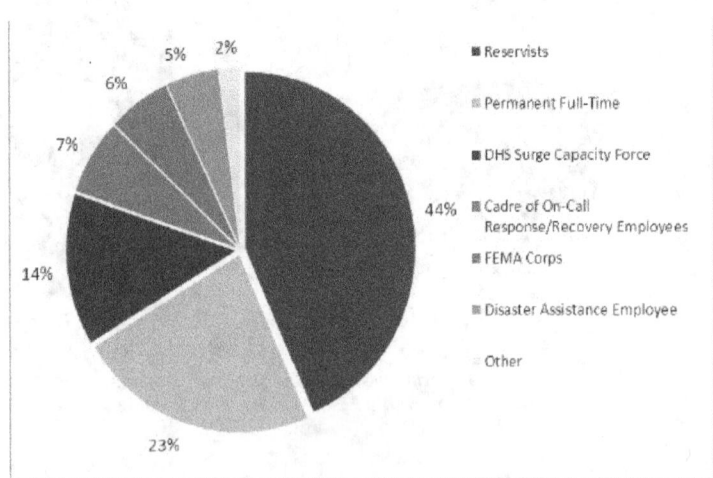

approximately 47 percent of positions required by the force structure being filled with qualified personnel, 25 percent were filled by trainees, and 28 percent remained vacant. Between 2013 and 2015, FEMA plans to make further investments in training, recruitment, and workforce management to address the gaps noted above and to ensure sufficient numbers of personnel are credentialed in positions required by force structure.

When Sandy occurred, FEMA was officially operating under FQS and the credentialing gaps noted above. Sandy provided a valuable opportunity to evaluate how FQS is transforming the FEMA workforce

Figure 19: The composition of FEMA's deployed workforce on November 19, 2012, indicates that FEMA deployed personnel from a wide range of sources.

into a more professional and deployable organization. The in-progress status of FQS implementation presented challenges to Sandy operations in the following ways:

- Thirty percent of deployed personnel did not have an FQS title and were assigned to positions they were not necessarily qualified to fill. This was especially problematic for PFT staff, 46 percent of whom were deployed without pre-assigned FQS titles.

- Those personnel who did have FQS titles did not always deploy to or stay in their positions. Twenty-eight percent of personnel who had FQS titles reported serving in roles outside their normal FQS position, and 32 percent reported changing roles over the course of their deployment.

- In order to ensure that disaster workforce personnel have sufficient opportunity to gain experience, new disaster workforce policies seek to prevent managers from requesting employees by name and, instead, fill positions based on a rotation model. However, 30 percent of Reservists who deployed to Sandy did so through by-name requests by JFO leadership. As of December 31, 2012, IWMD had agreed to 80 percent of these requests.

- FEMA has not completed the full alignment of FQS titles to actual positions required for response and recovery operations. For example, incident support roles such as those at the NRCC are still under development. Furthermore, some deployed personnel worked in roles that have no FQS titles (such as on the Innovation Team), while other FQS titles went unused.

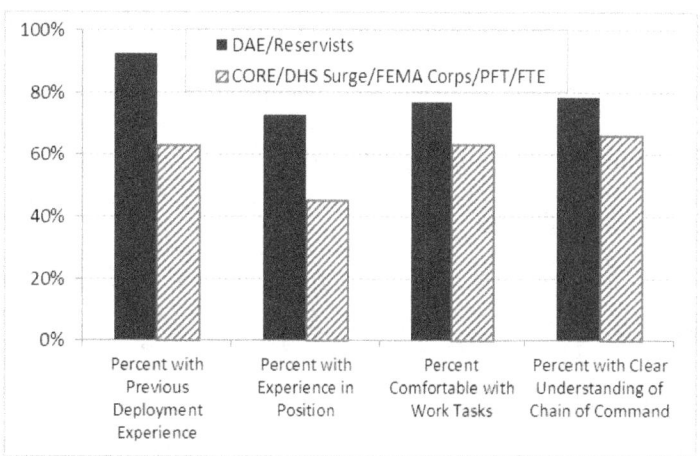

Figure 20: Personnel who were not traditionally part of the FEMA workforce had less experience and were less comfortable with their role.

- FEMA's permanent employees reported being less comfortable with their tasks than their Reservist counterparts (see Figure 20). Nearly all Reservists have an FQS title, and more than 90 percent of those deployed had prior deployment experience, compared to just over 60 percent among the deployed permanent workforce.

Because FQS launched shortly before Sandy, FEMA may adequately address the challenges noted above through planned activities in support of full implementation. However, in the interim, Sandy did reveal that FEMA may lack a coherent strategy to address temporary personnel shortfalls in specific FQS programs, especially for large-scale events.

Area for Improvement: Mobilizing the FEMA workforce for disaster response

Although FEMA completed one of the largest personnel deployments in its history, it nearly exhausted the number of available personnel. Moreover, staff who deployed for the first time—or without an assigned FQS title—reported confusion with deployment processes and expectations. By November 12, FEMA had only 355 Reservists (5 percent) available for potential deployment: 4,708 (67 percent) were already deployed to ongoing disasters, and 1,854 (26 percent) were unavailable. Such a high unavailability rate suggests that new leave policies for the Reservist Program may not have been fully enforced prior to Sandy. Furthermore, by November 12, FEMA had already deployed 2,221 (44 percent) of its permanent employees. Permanent FEMA employees filled a variety of roles during Sandy, including conducting Community Relations, staffing JFOs, working in the NRCC and RRCCs, and maintaining operations in their home offices while their colleagues were deployed. Because FEMA has approximately 5,000 permanent full-time employees and the Agency's force structure estimates that 2,500 of them are required to maintain operations outside of incident management requirements, the number of permanent employees deployed to Sandy appears to represent the vast majority available for deployment.

In addition, the Sandy response highlighted policy gaps regarding the deployment of the permanent workforce. FEMA's Automated Deployment Database (ADD) allows field leadership to request positions by FQS title and automatically contacts Reservists to deploy based on their requests. However, the ADD does not have the ability to automatically deploy members of the permanent workforce; rather, field leadership must make a specific by-name request for them. Among those surveyed, full-time-equivalent employees and managers reported confusion about deployment processes: 43 percent of PFTs reported that their deployment notification was ineffective. Moreover, some field staff reported confusion about how deployment requests should be prioritized among permanent, intermittent, and surge staff, especially given new Reservist Program policies that seek to offer equitable opportunities to gain the experience required for FQS qualification.

Together, these challenges indicate that opportunities exist to better prepare to deploy the entire workforce.

Area for Improvement: Supporting deployed personnel

Throughout the Sandy response, FEMA encountered difficulties supporting such a large deployed workforce. During the initial waves of personnel deployments, for instance, the Agency lacked a facility to stage personnel as they began deploying to the field. On November 1, FEMA established an ad hoc Personnel Staging Area (PSA) at Fort Dix, New Jersey, to address this need. FEMA used this facility to equip and organize staff before deploying them further afield to their assigned duty stations. The staging area operated for 14 days, processed 1,127 disaster workers, and provided over 6,300 nights of lodging. However, not enough planning went into the overall activation and operation of the PSA. For example, PSA staff at Fort Dix was unable to determine an accurate number of CR-AIR personnel that were going to require billeting each night. There was no tracking of departure of personnel en route to Fort Dix or to the New York reception facilities, even though a way to do so was identified in the field. Although FEMA has used PSAs successfully in the past, they require a great deal of logistic support and are not described in detail in current doctrine.

In addition to the challenges associated with the PSA, deployed personnel required some administrative and logistical services that FEMA had difficulty supporting. Many deployed personnel, especially non-FEMA employees in the DHS SCF, lacked information technology (IT) equipment, such as laptops, intranet access tokens, or smartphones. This prevented some staff from connecting to IT systems essential for their duties and from receiving updated instructions through email. In addition to IT equipment, many employees lacked appropriate apparel. Personnel working in the field, such as CR-AIR teams, lacked cold weather outerwear that identified them as FEMA personnel. In addition, some DHS SCF staff wore law enforcement agency apparel from their home DHS component, which were unsuited for the FEMA mission and may have deterred survivors from approaching them.

The response to Sandy also revealed challenges associated with lodging a large response force in densely populated areas. FEMA applied several innovative solutions to the lodging challenges, including housing personnel on U.S. Maritime Service ships and on a college campus and issuing waivers that increased allowable lodging expenses. While staff generally found these solutions to be effective, each of them was accompanied by its own set of implementation issues due to their ad hoc nature. These challenges indicate that FEMA's plans do not account for how the Agency will house a large deployed workforce.

Finally, the Agency faced a number of administrative challenges in supporting a large and diverse workforce. While Reservists have experience making travel and lodging arrangements and submitting timesheets and travel vouchers using one set of procedures, much of FEMA's permanent workforce was accustomed to using alternate procedures, which complicated the processing of timesheets and vouchers for the employees.

To help relieve the administrative burdens on deployed personnel, the New York JFO developed a Going Green initiative. This program found innovative solutions for administrative and financial inefficiencies experienced in the field, such as processing timecards electronically rather than with paper, and using public transportation instead of renting cars. In late 2012, IWMD, in collaboration with the Office of the Chief Component Human Capital Officer (OCCHCO), developed an electronic timekeeping pilot. This initiative, which was used in the New York and New Jersey JFOs, has assisted in the expedited processing of timecards for deployed Reservists. Even with these innovations, the challenges above indicate that opportunities remain to improve FEMA's support to its deployed personnel.

Area for Improvement: Ensuring continuity of operations

FEMA continuity of operations (COOP) planning—the continuation of Mission Essential Functions—has centered on scenarios in which FEMA facilities (such as Headquarters and Region offices) become unusable. This approach is directed by *Federal Continuity Directive 1*, approved by the White House National Security Staff, and signed by the Secretary of DHS.

The response to Sandy made it clear that FEMA COOP plans have not fully considered how the Agency should balance a large deployment of personnel with the need to maintain steady-state operations. For example, some managers were unable to make strategic decisions regarding which personnel they allowed to be deployed. As a result, certain components experienced difficulties performing their steady-state activities. Specific Sandy-related challenges included the following:

- FEMA components deployed staff to the field without considering their emergency relocation group responsibilities and how it would have impacted the Agency's ability to maintain continuity of government in the event of another disaster.

- The Office of the Chief Administrative Officer experienced backlogs in some programs, such as processing Freedom of Information Act requests.

- The Grant Programs Directorate experienced challenges in distributing its daily functions among its remaining staff, impacting communication with grant recipients.

- FEMA Regions experienced difficulties maintaining core functions. For example, Region VII deployed several IMAT members, which diminished the Region's capacity to respond to a disaster in its own region.

These experiences indicate that current continuity plans are not scalable and do not effectively position leaders to communicate their expectations for maintaining ongoing operations. Continuity plans do not contain options for levels of operations, or a framework for such levels. Additionally, the FEMA Headquarters (HQ) Continuity Plans and the Response Directorate family of disaster response plans are not synchronized and, therefore, may overlap or leave gaps in capabilities.

Conclusion

Sandy provided a significant test of FEMA's capabilities and those of its Whole Community partners. The scale and severity of the storm resulted in extensive effects—including flooding, damage to transportation networks and other critical infrastructure, power outages, fuel disruptions, and property damage—across the East Coast and inland. FEMA coordinated large-scale Federal response and recovery activities that contributed to the integrated, national effort to support affected communities.

While Sandy's effects were devastating, FEMA recognizes that it must plan for even larger, more severe storms and disasters. As FEMA prepares to respond to and recover from these larger scale incidents the strengths and areas for improvement identified in this report will help to guide the Agency.

In reviewing all aspects of the Agency's preparations for, immediate response to, and initial recovery from the storm, the Sandy Analysis Team identified strengths and areas for improvement organized across four overarching themes:

- Ensuring Unity of Effort Across the Federal Response;

- Being Survivor-Centric;

- Fostering Unity of Effort Across the Whole Community; and

- Developing an Agile, Professional Emergency Management Workforce.

In recognition of the importance of the findings in this report, FEMA has already begun to address a number of the areas for improvement. For example, FEMA has convened an Executive Steering Committee to update the mission assignment process and is adding functionality to its crisis management system to increase transparency of the status of mission assignments. The Agency also updated its *Incident Management Handbook* in January 2013 to clarify command relationships across its numerous field structures and enhance coordination with state, local, territorial, and tribal partners. Together with the ongoing focus of the CIWG, these actions demonstrate FEMA's commitment to learning lessons from response and recovery operations, developing solutions to identified issues, and following through on their implementation in the interest of better serving disaster survivors.

For many of the storm's survivors, recovery will be measured in years, not months. FEMA remains committed to working closely with the Whole Community to meet the long-term needs of survivors and to help the impacted states and communities to recover and rebuild.

Appendix 1: Acronym List

ADD	Automated Deployment Database
ARC	American Red Cross
CIWG	Continuous Improvement Working Group
CMS	Consumable Medical Supplies
COOP	Continuity of Operations
CORE	Cadre of On-Call Response/Recovery Employees
CR	Community Relations
CR-AIR	Community Relations-Assess, Inform, Report
DHAP	Disaster Housing Assistance Program
DHS	U.S. Department of Homeland Security
DIA	Disability Integration Advisor
DME	Durable Medical Equipment
DOD	U.S. Department of Defense
DRC	Disaster Recovery Center
ERG	Emergency Relocation Group
ESF	Emergency Support Functions
FCO	Federal Coordinating Officer
FEMA	Federal Emergency Management Agency
FIMA	Federal Insurance & Mitigation Administration
FPIC	FEMA Planning Integration Council
FQS	FEMA Qualification System
HMGP	Hazard Mitigation Grant Program
HUD	U.S. Department of Housing and Urban Development
IHP	Individual and Households Program
IMAT	Incident Management Assistance Team
IMH	Incident Management Handbook
IOF	Initial Operating Facility
IT	Information Technology
IWMD	Incident Workforce Management Division
IWMO	Incident Workforce Management Office
JFO	Joint Field Office
LL/CIP	Lessons Learned/Continuous Improvement Program
LMD	Logistics Management Directorate
LNO	Liaison Officer
LRO	Long Term Recovery Office
MERS	Mobile Emergency Response Support
MOTF	Modeling Task Force
NSP	National Support Plan
NBEOC	National Business Emergency Operations Center
NDRF	National Disaster Recovery Framework
NEMIS	National Emergency Management Information System
NFIP	National Flood Insurance Program
NISM	National Incident Support Manual

NPSC	National Processing Service Center
NRCC	National Response Coordination Center
NRF	National Response Framework
OCC	Office of Chief Counsel
OCCHCO	Office of the Chief Component Human Capital Officer
OCFO	Office of the Chief Financial Officer
OFA	Other Federal Agency
ORR	Office of Response and Recovery
PA	Public Assistance
PFT	Permanent Full-time
PSA	Personnel Staging Area
PSMA	Pre-Scripted Mission Assignment
RDIS	Regional Disability Integration Specialists
RRCC	Regional Response Coordination Center
RSF	Recovery Support Function
SCF	Surge Capacity Force
SOE	Senior Official Exercises
SOP	Standard Operating Procedure
STEP	Sheltering and Temporary Essential Power
TSA	Transitional Sheltering Assistance
UCG	Unified Coordination Group
USACE	U.S. Army Corps of Engineers
USCG	U.S. Coast Guard
VOAD	Volunteer Organization Active in Disasters

www.ingramcontent.com/pod-product-compliance
Lightning Source LLC
Chambersburg PA
CBHW080344290526
45791CB00009BA/2725